"The very afternoon I beg[] written on your life, my pop-[] Bible app came straight from R[omans 10]. [For it is with your heart] that you believe and are justified, and it is with your mouth that you profess your faith and are saved." Since we first met with Kristin at Demos' in downtown Nashville in 2013, I've experienced your testimony to this verse and, importantly, your journey from belief and profession of faith to know, love, and trust God and His will a little more every day. As a personal matter, I've felt the love of God through your personal outreach to me over the years, occasionally on one of my own dark or stressful days, and in your deep curiosity, vulnerability and openness—including the good times, the hard times and the confusing times—about God and His call on your life.

"As I read your book, *Afraid to Trust*, two things immediately struck me: how close your written story resembled having a deep personal conversation with a friend, new or old, about faith (your story reads like a personal journal and flies off the pages) and the examination, conviction, perseverance, joy, and hope you've experienced through a life moving toward God and His love. Even knowing some of your story, I felt all the more emboldened to see more clearly a loving God at work in my own life and to cleave more closely to discern His calling. And for those struggling with God, whether in belief, unbelief, or somewhere in between, your story gives context for the struggle—it's okay to ask questions, bear your soul, challenge, argue, and doubt. The Christian life is not easy street, but stories like yours bear testimony to a love, peace, and joy beyond comprehension for those whose hearts are moved to belief, whose mouths profess to faith, and whose persistent vision and actions are motivated by the love of God and an eternal life with Him."

—*Hank Flint, former President of Coca-Cola Bottling Company and current Vice President of the Board*

"I was captivated from the first chapter by the deep conversational tone so that I did not want to put the book down. Coming from a man who disliked Christians to making the decision to turn everything over to Him, God stripped away all the things that Peter had leaned on to trust God in his business and personal decisions. His story encourages new Christians to resist their fear and trust God while giving hope to those who have loved ones who have not yet seen a relationship with Christ. Peter, with humility, gives clear practical examples of how he has brought his faith to his work, how to be bold in the little things, and how to trust God to overcome his fear. His transparency makes his story compelling and shows that a Christian life is not easy but is secure knowing the love of God for those who believe."

—*Mark Whitacre, former FBI informant and current President of Operations at a biotechnology firm*

Afraid To Trust

One Man's Journey Into the Love of God

Peter Demos

Romulus, Michigan

Afraid To Trust

by Peter Demos

Unless otherwise identified, Scripture is taken from the New King James Version®, copyright ©1982 by Thomas Nelson, Inc. Used by permission. All rights reserved.

Scripture marked ESV are from the ESV® Bible (The Holy Bible, English Standard Version®), copyright ©2001 by Crossway, a publishing ministry of Good News Publishers. Used by permission. All rights reserved.

Scripture marked NIV are taken from *THE HOLY BIBLE: New International Version* ©1978 by the New York International Bible Society, used by permission of Zondervan Bible Publishers. All rights reserved.

ISBN 978-0-9988171-5-6

For Worldwide Distribution
Printed in the U.S.A.

FiveStonePress
Every Book a Giant-Killer
An imprint of Supernatural Truth Productions, LLC
www.FiveStonePress.com

Contents

Acknowledgments

I am grateful:

To my wife, Kristin, who never gave up on our marriage and turned to our Lord to save our marriage when I did not believe. Her strength and support, both public and private in the midst of the trials we face, give me hope and make me smile. Outside of Jesus, there is no one I love more or could even if I tried.

To my children, who each show me how Jesus can influence the youth. They are truly an inspiration.

To Angus Buchan, Ian Gray, Allen Jackson, and so many others who introduced me to the Holy Spirit and who continue to mentor me and provide time for my questions and rabbit holes I tend to crawl through.

To my ghost writer, Grace Schienbein, who was able to listen to my ramblings and capture my heart, my story, and my words in a way that I could never think was possible while keeping me on track. Her advice through this process was amazing

To God the Father, who loves us so much that He provided a plan for our rebellion against Him, even when it caused Him pain, and has given me the freedom to choose Him so my decision to follow His Son means so much more.

To Jesus, who chose me when I rejected Him, who cared enough to fight with me so I can see the light, who suffered for me, took my sins, took my sickness, took my shame, and who died for me so that I may live.

To the Holy Spirit, who guides me and comforts me. Who has healed me of many sicknesses. And who, through my relationship with Him, allows me to know my Lord and Savior on an intimate, relational level.

Introduction

When the second marriage counselor told me that I was afraid, I was angry. I was sure that I was not a fearful person, although I was someone who, under fits of rage, would attack anyone or anything that got in my way. This was fear, however, but I didn't know it until God took it away.

My fear showed in anger and avoidance, and it manifested itself in a petty meanness towards those that I cared about and in worse ways to those I did not. God removed this fear from me, but it tried to take over once again when everything seemed against me. But this time, instead of giving in to anger, I gave it over to God.

That phrase, easier shared as good advice than followed as a practical tool for most Christians, is the struggle I felt as I saw all the things that I had learned to lean on crumble around me. Years of business experience, friendships, and money were all stripped from me. As a result, I learned I could experience real fear and then use the antidote to this disease—trusting in God and continuing to submit my business and business decisions to Him as the real managing Director of my business.

As I have spoken to secular and Christian groups, I have seen so many people crying about their lives and their feelings of hopelessness when it appears that so much greatness is going on around them. God is the only true hope. This story, which was awful as I went through it, hopefully will serve as an encouragement to those who are lost, Christians that are struggling, and for Christians who want to do more in the marketplace but are either afraid to take the first step or unsure how to do so.

My story takes you down the road of how a church-going

child can turn against Christians, become an adult and find Jesus, and then try to understand His love as he struggles with turning over his life to the one Person who loves him more than anyone has ever attempted to.

Learning to trust God means you have to accept His love and no longer be...*Afraid To Trust*

ONE

Coming Clean

It had been a long time coming, I suppose. When I finally broke, it wasn't in a couple of pieces, easily repairable. I was completely shattered. The old Peter wasn't coming back. I knelt naked before God, not metaphorically but literally on my knees, sobbing in the shower with water pounding against my back, and steam swirling around me. The last few days in Memphis amounted to the labor pains of a particularly difficult spiritual birth.

When I stepped into that hotel shower, I was exhausted. I had come to the city for the Tennessee Hospitality Association's quarterly board meeting of four days and three nights of seminars and meetings. I normally quite enjoyed these events, talking shop with like-minded men and women. I didn't particularly love that this particular meeting was held in Memphis. I've joked in the past that if Tennessee gave Memphis to Arkansas, both states would improve.

I went to school for two years in Memphis, and I am not joking when I say that they were quite possibly the worst two years of my life. Just after I moved there, my high school sweetheart broke up with me. I found myself incredibly lonely and ended up getting involved with a bad crowd.

A lot of kids do things they regret in their first year or two of college, and I was one of them. I found out that girls plus a credit card with a high limit plus a lonely kid away from parental supervision equals huge debt, terrible grades, and bad choices. When I transferred colleges to Middle Tennessee State University two years later, I found I had to repeat some of the classes. I had spent two years of school in a place I hated and had little to show for it.

It's kind of funny to me now that Memphis, of all places, is where God finally got hold of me. I left for the conference in Memphis straight from a church meeting in Nashville, which in and of itself was an oddity; I wasn't exactly a churchgoing man. Church and I never really got along.

I was the kid who was kicked out of Sunday School for challenging the teacher. I was the teen who would tease and bully the Christian kids at school. I was the man who insisted business and faith shouldn't mix and chastised employees who thought differently. I could think of a million other places I would rather be on a Sunday than sitting through a church service.

When my wife, Kristin, had insisted I join her to listen to a special speaker at church, I initially resisted, but Kristin was adamant. Things had been tense enough at home that I figured I should capitulate on this one. Over the next two days, I ended up attending two church services and a separate church meeting, and responding to an altar call. I didn't know what was happening to me and I didn't like it.

I was a little ticked off with myself for responding to that altar call at the Sunday service. I was even angrier when a random question from the guest speaker, Angus Buchan, at a special breakfast on Monday morning haunted me all the way from Nashville to Memphis, especially when I shouldn't have been at that breakfast meeting anyway!

The drive took about four hours from church to hotel. I left that church breakfast with a strange feeling in my chest. Angus Buchan's question created in me an internal struggle—a tug-of-war between conviction over how I was living my life and a desire to retain control. The question Mr. Buchan had asked me was, "Why would you be willing to die for your country, but you aren't willing to speak up for God?" I honestly wondered what was keeping me from doing that.

I believed in God in my own way, even when I didn't want to, but after years of questioning and never seeming to get any answers, I decided for myself that God was an absentee landlord. He didn't really seem to get involved with what we were up to, and if we didn't bother Him, He wouldn't bother us. But now I was starting to doubt my own ill-informed beliefs.

I was willing to fight for a lot of things. I would fight for my business; I would fight for my family; I would fight for what I felt was true. If God was real, and if what the speaker and the pastor had been saying about Him the last couple of days was correct, what kept me from living for Him?

After about an hour and a half, I started to realize I wouldn't be able to figure out what this Christian thing was really about on my own. I downloaded an app from the church and started listening to sermons, flipping to any title that caught my attention.

There was one that stuck with me more than many of the others. The sermon was talking about the lives of Jesus' disciples and more specifically about the life of Thomas, who may have doubted early on but ended well. I had heard stories about the disciples as a kid. Back then, if asked, I would have said I wanted to be like Peter. Peter was a man of action.

He was the one who got to walk on water. He was the one who would cut off a guy's ear to defend Jesus. Sure, he was hot-headed and did the wrong thing a lot of the time, but he was a fighter. Unfortunately, I knew I wasn't a Peter. Even then I figured I was more like Thomas—I had all sorts of questions and no answers. That left me plagued with doubt.

Allen Jackson (the pastor of our church, not Alan Jackson, the country singer) is a very considerate, eloquent man and a thinker. On occasion, he would say something that would strike me, and I would have to pause and reflect on how it applied to my life. I kept on listening to his sermons for the rest of the drive.

I arrived at my hotel just as frustrated as I had been during the four hours it took to get there from Nashville. I checked in and headed for my room. To be honest, I just needed to hide away for a while. I wanted to take back control of my brain, but I couldn't. I couldn't think about anything but finding out the truth about God.

Was Pastor Allen a hack? Was he some master manipulator, knowing just the right words to use to create an emotional response? I got on my computer and started to investigate. My years as a lawyer had taught me how to research. I knew if I tried hard enough, I would find something on him. And I thought the special speaker who had somehow gotten me out of my seat in the middle of a row of chairs to respond to an altar call I didn't really want to respond to was surely some sort of hypnotist.

When I had to go to my first meeting, I left my hotel room feeling anxious to get back. When the meeting was over, I didn't stick around to schmooze with the other guests like I used to; I high-tailed it back to my room. I usually would have gone out for dinner and drinks with some of the other longstanding members of the Tennessee Hospitality Association who were friends I only saw a few times a year. But that night I couldn't stand to make small talk or even pretend to be interested.

I went back to my room and ordered room service. I felt tired since it had been a long weekend and a long drive. It was late and I had a full day of meetings on Tuesday. I finished eating and flopped back on my king-sized bed and tried to get comfortable. I turned over again and again. It's impossible to lie still when your brain is busy. I turned over on the right side of the bed and swung my legs over the side; from there I could work at the desk if I wanted. I flipped my laptop screen back on and pulled up another sermon.

For nearly the entire night, I listened to more sermons by my pastor, I watched interviews with well-known Christians, like Kirk Cameron and Angus Buchan, and I spent hours researching evolution. After listening to someone or something particularly convicting, I would then look them up to see if there was anything to discredit them. I really hoped there was.

Tuesday's meetings were exhausting. I felt increasingly uncomfortable being away from my room. I didn't really know what was going on with me, I just felt compelled to be there.

Wednesday was much the same. I would go to the meetings I had to be at and skipped everything else. In the three nights I was there, I slept a maximum of four hours. Most of the night was spent looking up what it means to live the Christian life. Every night I struggled on my own, researching, wrestling with God, and flopping from side to side on the bed. I got up again and again to watch sermons on YouTube or read articles from Christians on what it means to be a Christian and what I had to do if I chose to follow Christ.

Thursday morning I was a wreck. I had one final board meeting before my drive back to Nashville. I was in that kind of exhausted state where your body tries to sleep a little every time you blink. Getting dressed felt like a huge effort. I had no idea how I would manage the four-hour drive back to Nashville on one of the world's more boring roads. Everyone in Tennessee agrees that the drive on I-40 sucks, and that's when you are awake.

I decided to hop in the shower, hoping the water would wake me up. There was now one other worry fighting for attention in my brain—how on earth was I going to get home without killing myself?

The water pounding on my back did little to end my exhaustion. In the shower, my thoughts vacillated between getting home in one piece and how I could live a Christian life. After all my research the last few days, it seemed almost impossible for any man. As I fought, it was like God fought back. The mental battle was excruciating. Finally, God broke me.

I cried out, "You win! I turn everything over to You." Suddenly I had this feeling unlike anything I had ever experienced before, not even when I had answered the altar call a few days before. It felt like something entered me from above, and with a swoop, grabbed all the darkness in me and lifted it up and out the other side. It was as if skillful, unseen hands had swept through me and removed the cancer of sin in my life. I hadn't even been aware that I was so much a slave to sin and fear until God took it away. I didn't realize what a control issue I had until I gave control over to God.

When that happened, I dropped to my knees sobbing. But I wasn't crying from sadness or remorse. I was sobbing with joy; all these amazing emotions were spilling over. I was literally overcome with a joy so full that I felt like my mortal body couldn't handle it for long. I felt like the Grinch whose heart grew two sizes that day, bursting out of that little x-ray frame. I was too overwhelmed to remain upright.

As I stepped out of the shower, I noticed that all my senses seemed heightened, both physical and emotional. I felt like I could see and hear more clearly than ever before. Colors seemed more vibrant. Everything was fresh and clean—I was a new man! The exhaustion I was feeling from lack of sleep completely left me. I got dressed and packed with a spring in my step.

I went to that final board meeting excited to see everyone. These people that I had known the last few years, but I saw only occasionally, suddenly became very dear to me. I loved them, I bounded up to them and gave them hugs with a huge grin on my face. I'm sure I looked like some schoolboy in the first throws of love, and they probably wondered why a person who hated to touch or even sit close to others was hugging people and slapping them on the back.

I don't remember texting my wife, but she tells me she wondered what was up because I kept sending her these lovey-dovey texts out of the blue. In fact, I apparently was texting her so much, telling her how much I loved her and how amazing I thought she was, that it started to really annoy her. As I look back on it, I think that she was obviously the first person God wanted me to reconcile with. Kristin and I hadn't been in a good place; I can see now that God was already working to restore that relationship.

I hadn't even been aware that I was carrying that much fear and insecurity. Others viewed me as a fighter; a man who spoke his mind and micro-managed others through intimidation. Most people who knew me, including my family, didn't see me as a man who was afraid. I wasn't even aware of the fear in my life even when our marriage counselor out-and-out told me that I was afraid of losing my wife and had become so jealous I almost pushed her away. It was only after Jesus took it away that I realized how much fear I had.

Two

Dealing With Christians

I was sinful from birth. We all are. I believe that now. But I'm aware that my heart became harder and more rebellious towards God and His people the older I got. That hard, rebellious heart is at the root of sin, and it taught me to pull away from a God I believed existed but didn't like overly much.

Like many other sinners, I grew up going to church. The church I first remember attending was in a beautiful structure. It was the type you would find in the background of bridal magazines. Its tall steeple and gleaming white walls paired perfectly with well-manicured lawns and green trees, perched on a hill that overlooked a main street in Brentwood, Tennessee.

I can still remember the feel of the smooth wooden pews that were older than any of the congregants. I remember how it felt to slide back and forth on them in my Sunday best, trying to find a way to keep my bony backside from going numb. It was an Episcopal church, a denomination my parents could both agree on attending but one in which my mother never felt completely at ease.

My dad, Jim Demos, was raised Greek Orthodox. He appreciated that the priest there still wore robes and led a weekly communion, a practice that is still very important to him.

My mom, Doris, was a sharecropper's daughter, literally born in a cotton field and baptized in a muddy river in Georgia. She was raised about as Southern Baptist as they come; as a result, she had a lot of negative things to say about that particular denomination.

The Episcopal church seemed to hit just the right balance between the two denominations and so that is how my sister and I grew up. There were lots of sitting, standing, and kneeling. You were expected to know what to do and when to do it, which I never seemed to really get the hang of. Now I think they give you directions in the church bulletin. Having to watch others in order to know what to do, however, was more interesting than reciting the words from the Book of Common Prayer.

The worst was always the long portion of the service where you had to kneel. My knees would feel like they were burning well before we were ever allowed to sit back on the pew. I would sneak a glance over at my dad to see if he was watching, and if he had his eyes on the pastor, I would lean back against the pew.

But my dad must have had a sixth sense because no sooner had I leaned back than I would feel a hard smack on the back of the head and catch my dad's forbidding eyes zeroing in on me. I guess he thought if you were touching the pew during kneeling time, it was tantamount to cursing out the priest while he gave the blessing.

I couldn't wait for the benediction to let us all know we could go. In fact, my first memory of church was the priest giving the benediction and walking down the long center aisle to the front doors. His hands were folded in front of him, and his robe was swishing back and forth with each long step. As soon as he reached the doors, everyone filtered out of those long narrow pews and made their way towards the exit to shake his hand.

It was exciting to be finally at the end of the service. I was practically dancing in my spot in line, waiting to get out the doors. I bet my dad was just as eager to get out of there so he could go to work. We usually went to the eight o'clock service. There was another at half past ten, but Dad had his restaurant to think of. Sundays are busy days for restaurant owners.

In my memory, I can still recall the priest's face and his tone of voice as I held out my little hand to his. He shook it kindly and looked up at the next person in line. But one day I wasn't ready to let go. There was something bothering my five-year-old brain. I stared up at him and said, with all earnestness, "I can't understand how God can be everywhere."

To his credit, he didn't just shoo me along, despite the line up of people now stalled behind me. He bent low and said in an almost conspiratorial tone, "Imagine sitting in a room with toys all around you." I did imagine it. He carried on, "All the toys are there, but you can't see them all, can you? There are some behind you, outside of your vision."

He smiled beatifically at me, and my mom hustled me out the doors. Even at the age of five, I thought it was a dumb answer. I just had to turn my head to see the toys behind me. But no matter how many times I turned my head, I couldn't see God. How could we ever know if He was actually everywhere or not? Maybe He was nowhere.

I wasn't finding any answers at Sunday School either. My class back then was taught by a husband and wife team. To be honest, I can't remember much about the wife at all, but I do know I liked the man that was teaching us; he was wonderfully nice.

He looked pretty much like your average businessman of the 70s. Salt and pepper hair combed to the side with long thick sideburns. He wore wide-lapelled suits and would always talk to me about the Dallas Cowboys, my favorite team. He would chat happily with me about the latest game and taught me about how divisions and the NFL playoffs work. That was really the only thing I learned there that stuck with me.

Most Sundays Dad couldn't stick around after the service, so Mom would let us skip Sunday School altogether. She would take me instead to have breakfast somewhere, and that was really alright with me. Sunday School was in between the two morning services, so during that time, the church was always full of people. I liked escaping the crowd and getting something to eat.

Our time at the bright white church with the giant steeple ended when I was about seven or eight years old. My sister, who was a teenager in the late 70s, informed my parents that her Sunday School teacher was telling the girls that they should be getting birth control. You can imagine my rural Southern Baptist mother's reaction. This would be a big deal now, but back then it was huge.

"That's it!" my mom said firmly, "we are leaving this church. They have no right to tell you…" Her voice caught. She was fuming. It was outrageous. How dare someone else tell her daughter to go on birth control?

The next Sunday we tried out a Presbyterian church. It seemed similar in some ways to the Episcopal, but there were some glaring differences too. The building itself was an attractive construction made of brick. It was much larger than our last church and had a gorgeous circular drive that went all the way around to the back. We found out on our first Sunday there that this church also had a school and my parents thought it would be a good idea if I went there.

I soon was registered for the fourth grade and looking forward to going. I was pretty popular in the third grade at public school, so I assumed people would love me in the fourth grade at a private Christian school.

I walked down the long hallway on that first day to the outside portables where fourth grade was held, nervous but hopeful. I was glad that it wasn't hard to find my way around. There was only one level to this school, and all the classrooms were also used for Sunday School, so I had even been in them before. I knew exactly what to expect from the old wooden desks complete with inkwells to the kids who should be avoided at all costs.

Any hope that I had that I would remain a cool kid in this school quickly vanished. The kids in this Christian school were much meaner than the ones in the public school I had left. These kids didn't just call you names—they practiced the fine art of snobbery. They knew just how to ostracize someone for maximum impact. They had particularly cold shoulders pointed my way.

It wasn't just bullying from students that I had to deal with either. Teachers also got in on the fun. These "Christian" teachers would pick favorites. If you weren't the teacher's pet, you were no better than a diseased rodent.

I quickly learned to hate that school and everything about it. It used to be that the weekends meant a break from the teachers and students that picked on you; unfortunately for

me, my school was also my church. I would get a double
dose of the kids and teachers that went there.

I can't imagine a less Christian, Christian school than the
one attached to that church. Any form of Christ-likeness was
abandoned at its doors. There I learned about evolution, and
it was taught as fact. One period out of every day was for
Bible class, which was taught by an old, matronly woman
with grey hair and a pinched face. I don't remember her
name, but I can't forget how her pantyhose would droop and
sag around her ankles. She always wore patterned dresses
that stopped just below the knee.

She would settle herself down on a chair, and we would
sit on the floor in front of her as she read stories from pretty
much any book but the Bible. All the while my eyes would
watch the wrinkles of her pantyhose shift above her sensible
shoes, like undulating waves against the shore.

I spent just over two years in that terrible place until in
grade six, I had a teacher so miserable my mother had pity on
me. This teacher, in particular, hated all boys. Her smile for
the girls in the class would disappear as soon as a male of the
species gained her attention. She was the kind of teacher who
would give favorite students (in this case, the girls) points for
answers that were "close enough" but take away points from
a boy whose answer was sloppy, or who had something in the
wrong spot.

After months of telling my mom what was happening at
the school, she went to have a word with that teacher. She
generally sided with authority, which meant I lost most battles when complaining about the state of things to my mother.
She was sure it was just some oversight, and the teacher
couldn't possibly hold such a bias. She was wrong, and it

didn't take her long into the conversation to figure that out. Her final words to the teacher as she realized that I was going to have to finish a hard year there was, "Thank you."

As the teacher looked at her confused, my mother continued, "Thank you for teaching Peter that life is not fair. Now that he's learned that, I don't believe there is anything else that you can teach him."

It wasn't long after that there was a break up in the church, and after following the new pastor for a couple of months, we returned to the Episcopal church. We didn't go to Sunday School very much anymore anyway, but I did start attending the church youth group.

Unfortunately, I can't say the kids there were any better than the Christian kids at my old school. I joined them for an overnight youth retreat, and it was one of the worst weekends of my life. It's hard enough being a pubescent boy, it's even worse when you are one of the ones continually excluded from all activities.

They took us to a camp out in the middle of nowhere. The bus ride there was a hint of what was to come. I had no one to sit with. I told myself it was no big deal. I had brought a book so I didn't need anyone to talk to. A loner, reading a book is an easy target for people wanting to practice droll observations.

"You're reading a book?"

I nodded.

"Let's see it."

I held up the cover. A dumb thing to do.

"Hahaha, how old are you? I read that years ago."

More laughter. My face flamed red and I sank down further in my seat.

"Hey guys, guess what Peter's reading…"

Holding back angry tears is difficult. They choke you. But I did.

Later, as an adult, I realized that it was unlikely that any elementary student had read that book. It's even above grade level for most junior high kids. It was just a 14-year-old boy's way of making another boy feel insignificant, and it worked. I did feel like a stupid, worthless, nothing—a big ol' zero.

When we finally got to the camp, I couldn't get off the bus fast enough. It was a picturesque spot with a smattering of cabins. I found mine and dumped my things on an empty bunk. The other guys laughed and joked and pretended I wasn't there. I told myself I didn't care. I didn't want to hang out with them anyway.

But perversely, somehow I still did. I wanted to be noticed and accepted. I wanted to have private jokes and laugh about someone else's weird habits. Instead, I escaped the cabin and went wandering. I only joined the group when it was time to eat or sleep. No one seemed to care. No one came up to me to ask how I was doing or to invite me to join them. My experience that weekend established the fact that Christian kids, in general, were mean.

It wasn't just Christian kids either. I noticed that Christian adults could be that way too. My family wasn't going to Sunday School anymore, but we did occasionally head to the fellowship area after the service. We didn't do much fellow-shipping though. It seemed like most of the people there ignored my entire family. Why were Christians such jerks?

My parents sent me to a private high school with Christian values. The values seemed about as Christian as the ones I had seen at the previous Christian school I attended. The only blatantly Christian thing about the school, as far as I could tell, was morning devotions. Every student in ninth grade was required to do a devotional at least once during the school year. It was my first public speaking experience. Not only did I have to speak in front of the four hundred people that made up our student body. I had to talk to them about the Bible.

I walked to the front of the auditorium, my whole body shaking. Before I even got one word out, I knocked my notecards over the side of the podium both onto the stage and down on the floor of the auditorium. I couldn't think of anything remotely witty or self-effacing to say about it either because of the butterflies in my stomach. I thought I might vomit. As I started to pick the notecards up, my shoulder hit the podium and it tipped over. Four hundred students started laughing at my misfortune.

I finally got my notecards together and righted the podium. I held on to it with shaking hands and kept my eyes fixed on those little rectangles of paper, now horribly out of order. When I finally found my voice, it cracked badly. I sped through the reading of a few cards and ran off the stage as fast as was humanly possible. I raced into the next room and threw up. I was so shaken and so weak from the experience, I vowed I would never speak in public again. Why would anyone voluntarily submit themselves to that kind of trauma? By eleventh grade, the constant taunting and bullying from both students and the teachers became too much to take. I couldn't even finish out the school year; I transferred halfway through to a public school. This time, I decided, I was going to do my best to make friends. I walked into the lunchroom that first day and sat down with a group that would prove not to be the best influence. It's almost a cliché, isn't it of the shy loner becoming a part of the bad crowd.

When the history club went on an overnight field trip to Shiloh National Battlefield, it was my first experience away from home with kids that actually wanted me around. When the teachers had all gone to bed, my new friends and I snuck out under cover of darkness. We headed down to Pickwick Lake where one of the guys brought out a bottle of vodka we had snuck in. Actually, he bought it and I smuggled it in because I had luggage that locked.

I was a little worried about breaking the law and drinking underage, but I didn't want to be the only one sitting there not drinking. When the bottle got to me, I took a little swig. It burned and tasted awful. Why would anyone voluntarily drink that stuff? When the bottle came around again, I faked another swig. Around and around that bottle went. I had a sneaking suspicion I wasn't the only guy pretending to partake. There was only one guy in the whole group who seemed to really be drinking. He was the odd man out.

In too short a time, this guy had drunk most of the bottle, and he was wasted. He got up and stumbled toward the water. And then there was a splash—he had fallen in. It was early spring, but the water must have been crazy cold.

One of the other guys and I ran over and tried to pull him out. It wasn't easy; the lake was surrounded by saplings, and the cold weather made them stiffer to push through than they might have been otherwise. When we finally pulled him free, we realized that the saplings had torn up his stomach quite severely, and his skin was icy cold.

We found his roommate and told him to come and take

him back to their room. This guy was a few bricks shy of a load, let me tell you. He took him back and stuck him in a cold bath in order "to sober him up." Instead, he made him hypothermic. It almost killed him. Most of us had gone back to our rooms and planned to stay there. But when the teachers found out one of their students was in such rough shape he needed to be taken to a hospital, they went looking for answers.

One of the teachers had seen me eating with the guy earlier in the day. "You were with him, weren't you? Where did you get the alcohol? Did you make him drink it?"

I wasn't eager to get in trouble, but I admitted that I'd been with him that night.

"And who else was there. It wasn't just the two of you, was it?"

It's one thing to admit to my misdeeds, but I wasn't interested in losing my new friends by ratting them out. No, I wouldn't do it.

Not a smart move. My parents were called, even though it was one in the morning, and were asked to pick me up. The school informed them that I was expelled. My mom and dad were livid, and rightly so. It wasn't what they wanted to hear in the middle of the night.

It didn't take long for rumors to circulate, and in short order, they guessed who the rest of the group was. When I confirmed their suspicions, they agreed to downgrade my expulsion to a twenty-day suspension.

The principal came to talk to me after a few days. "You seem like a good kid, Peter, why would you choose to hang out with kids that are leading you down this path?"

I didn't have a good answer for him.

"There are other groups in the school. Clubs you can join. What about that Christian group?"

I laughed, "Honestly, sir? It's because there are way too many drugs in those groups, and I don't want anything to do with them." He looked a little surprised, but he didn't push.

I wasn't lying to him either. The so-called Christian groups in the school did have a high number of drug users. I was firm in my belief that Christian kids were the biggest hypocrites out there. Despite that, if asked I still identified myself as a Christian. After all, I had gone to church most of my life, what else was I?

This past week, I had three people tell me that they don't want to have anything to do with Christianity due to Christians and at that moment, I just wanted to let them know that I get it. I really do. I spent many years making that same argument. (A quick Google search will give you great ideas on how to respond to this with grace and wisdom.)

Colossians 4:6 says, "Let your speech be gracious, seasoned with salt, so that you ought to know how to answer each person."

Despite my experiences, the rejection of Christians and Christianity was strictly on my shoulders. It had more to do with my own rebellion than it did other Christians. I used all sorts of avenues to justify my hard heart. But now, as a Christian, I hate the idea that I might in any way contribute to someone's distorted view of God.

THREE

Payback

"Vengeance is mine, I will repay, says the Lord" (Romans 12:19).

That verse is the worst, isn't it? At least, I wish sometimes that it never existed. Sometimes, I would just like to have the means and opportunity to get a little retribution against the people that have wronged myself or my family. But when I let God take control of a situation and hold back on repaying evil for evil, my faith and love of God grow. I see Him fight for me. I know what the enemy tries to do to destroy me is the very thing God uses to build me up and teach me.

I am also extremely glad that God is merciful because there are plenty of things in my past that deserved His vengeance. As is the case for most of us, my misdeeds started small. Being a "Christian" myself didn't stop me from trying to get a rise out of other Christian kids. At first, I tried out some light teasing and taunting. If one of them said, "I'll pray for you," I'd respond, "Don't bother."

I found a little bit of pleasure in seeing them turn red and look flustered. Some of them got angry; some were embarrassed. Turning the tables on them felt good. It was entertaining. I liked to see them stutter and stammer and not have any answers. After all, I wasn't saying anything bad about God when I attacked Christians. And we're supposed to do what makes us happy, right?

Soon I had honed my response so that it would be just a little more cutting. I'd say, "If God doesn't know when I need help, then He doesn't get to be God." Some of them would try and fumble through an explanation about the importance of prayer, but most of them would give up after I summarily dismissed them. I think they realized what I was trying to do. My challenge was basically "pick your poison." If they just walked away without defending their faith, they looked bad. If they tried to argue that God did indeed know everything, then why should we pray?

One day, one of the kids in my grade got into a car accident. I saw that he had one of those corn-ball "God is my co-pilot" bumper stickers. I laughed at him and said, "If that's true, He isn't doing a very good job."

I loved the reaction I would get by calling out their hypocrisy. I looked clever and funny. Other classmates seemed to like it too. The laughs and the snickers made me do it more and more. It felt like a justifiable form of retribution.

And when they would quote, "Vengeance is mine sayeth the Lord," I'd respond with the quote from the *Dirty Dozen*, "But it doesn't limit Him to the tools He uses, now does it?" I would mock and challenge any type of Christian speak. I was the bully for a change, and Christians were an easy target.

My view on God and Christianity began to warp in high school, but it was in college when I really went on the attack. I became fascinated with the Scopes Monkey Trial, in which a Tennessee teacher, John Thomas Scopes, was accused of teaching evolution in a State school, which was illegal at the time. The trial became famous for presenting a logical and legal argument for evolution.

It was like a handbook for someone like me. I read the transcript, watched documentaries, watched the fictional account, *Inherit the Wind*, both film versions and several live theatres. I idolized Clarence Darrow for his brilliance in shutting down what I saw was an ancient tradition of worship, proven wrong by basic scientific research.

While I was still a student at Memphis State, I met a girl who seemed pretty fantastic. She was a Christian, but I wouldn't hold that against her. When she invited me to join her at the Christian Students Center, I readily agreed. To their credit, the people there were super nice, maybe a little too nice. In my pretentious, college boy, know-it-all way of thinking, they appeared weak. They weren't outspoken on anything and gave up quickly if challenged.

The pastor at the center asked me if I would like to do a Bible study. No one had asked me that before. I was actually kind of interested, so I agreed to meet with him once a week with the idea that he and I would go through a couple of chapters together each session.

That first day we met, I was eager to dive in. His office was a small little room off to the side of a giant rec room. Its size made it feel like a safe space to ask the questions that had pressed in on me since childhood.

We started reading in the gospels. We got a few verses in when I had a question. He calmly and patiently answered, and we moved on. We got a few more verses in, and I stopped him with another. In a short amount of time, I realized I was aggravating him.

I was asking strong, hard, logical questions. I wasn't trying to be mean or annoying, I really was trying to learn, but I don't think the pastor knew that. With each interruption, he started to get more aggressive in his responses. The more aggravated he became, and the more abrupt his answers, the more aggravated I became. By the third week of our study, he blew up at me, "If it's written down, I believe it. End of story."

End of story? Really? Obviously, I knew he meant specifically things written in the Bible, but I just had to expose how ridiculous he just sounded. "So, you also believe in Greek mythology then?" I asked.

That was it. The pastor threw me out, and I was encouraged not to return.

After leaving Memphis State, due to some bad choices in my life, I moved to Murfreesboro to attend Middle Tennessee State University. There, again because of a girl, I started attending an adult Sunday School.

Again, I started in with my questions. The Sunday School teacher, an older woman, tall and thin with short curly hair and a church-lady, floral dress finally confronted me. In a tone that brooked no more nonsense, she said, "You're asking too many questions that I don't think we can answer, so it would probably be best if you don't come back."

By this time it was the early 90s. Televangelists had gained immense popularity, and the scandals made national news. It was the perfect ammunition for my attack on Christianity. These celebrity Christians with huge followings were frauds.

If I wanted to shut someone up, I would point to these Christian men and women who were famously hypocritical. I would quote "reliable" sources like tabloid newspapers but argue with such vigor that they appeared as credible as a scholarly journal.

Further, I had a much better time hanging out with my atheist and agnostic friends. They weren't just uncertain or disbelieving of God's existence; they were strongly anti-Christian. Through my talks with them, I started to find some common ground. We would sit around listening to death metal music and joke that we'd rather spend eternity with those who were going to hell than with those who were going to heaven.

At that time, I concluded that faith was the absence of logic, and so I wanted nothing to do with it. And yet, in my heart, I still kind of thought there might be a God. Based on the problems in the world and my understanding of Christians, I told myself He was probably a jerk, and I didn't want anything to do with Him.

If God was a jerk, there was no reason to show Him any respect. A lot of my atheist friends were on the debate team with me. We would regularly debate the Christian kids from our team as well as other schools outside of rounds, attempting and more often succeeding to trip them up and make them look foolish.

The hotel Bibles were an effortless way to aggravate them. On one of our team trips, we grabbed the Gideon Bible from beside the bed and used it as a doorstop because the hotel would not let us use the deadbolt to hold a door open anymore.

On another trip, I took the Bible and threw it off the balcony into the parking lot while a Christian guy on the team watched. My friends and I laughed at the look of shock on his face; it was payback for all the times Christians had made me feel like that or worse.

By the time I was in law school, I had settled down a bit. I would still argue with Christians about evolution, the virgin birth, and the real meaning of Jesus' parables, but I didn't aggressively seek them out. I wasn't any closer to making God a part of my life, but I didn't have to be such a jerk about it.

I finally settled on this "fact" about God: God is an absentee landlord. He's up there. I'm down here. If the pipes burst, He might do something to help me out, but otherwise probably not. I just had to make sure to pay Him rent once in a while.

That's the guy I was when I met Kristin. She was another nice Christian girl, Southern Baptist through and through. When I married her, I married into a family that had several Southern Baptist preachers and members who were actively involved in ministry. But I wasn't going to let that bother me. I loved her and she loved me; for her sake, I would rise above. For the most part, I was fine completely ignoring God and those who loved Him.

I thank God now that He was keeping me. Even though I had been hurt by many Christians in the past, there were always a few, like Kristin, that I loved and that I knew loved me. Despite all the off-putting experiences with the church, there was something in me that still believed He existed and wanted to believe that He is good.

I feel bad for the way I attacked Christians in the past. But now, as a follower of Christ, I knew that I could expect to be attacked. Jesus reminded His disciples that if the world hates them, to keep in mind it hated Him first (see John 15:18).

As a bearer of His name, I need to be careful about my response. In 1 Peter 3:15 we are instructed to give an answer for the hope that we have with gentleness and respect. Arguing will only incite more ridicule and push them further from the truth. It was simple for me to provoke Christians in the past, but when I found I couldn't, I developed a respect for them even while I tried to avoid them. I could not use their words and how they responded as an excuse.

FOUR

Baby Steps

Looking back, I can see how God was drawing me even though I fought Him tooth and nail.

One of those little indicators that God is at work in the life of an unbeliever is when He surrounds him with Christians. He did that for me. Despite how mean I was to many of them, there were still a large number of Christians who hung around me.

Even when I tried to surround myself with friends who were agnostics or atheists, there were always Christians around me that allowed me to abuse them. They not only let me say all sorts of vile things about their beliefs, they still selflessly chose to love me.

One of them was my best friend since I was fifteen. She prayed consistently for me to come to Christ, and when we were older, she also prayed for me to find a Christian wife. I am so grateful that she did. Out of all my Christian friends and acquaintances, my wife, Kristin, was the most significant influence on me.

No matter how I questioned, no matter how I revolted against organized religion, Kristin never wavered in her faith. She was okay with our believing separate things if it meant that her faith wasn't compromised.

Once we had children, I felt duty-bound to go to church with her and the kids. I figured they should have to suffer as I did in the same way it was my duty to make them eat vegetables. Kristin wanted to find a church that fit our whole family, and so she found a place she enjoyed that also had a great kids program.

Enjoying church was a novel concept to me. I just didn't understand how anyone would choose to go for any reason other than obligation. I usually felt pretty miserable sitting there in my exit row seat, waiting for the final amen. Generally, I would go with Kristin to church only when I couldn't find an excuse not to. And although I would concede that the pastor's sermons were sort of interesting sometimes, it was still like voluntary torture most Sundays. Oddly though, if I managed to evade going to church for a few months, I inexplicably wanted to go back. I honestly couldn't explain the desire, but there was something in me that compelled me to return.

God didn't just use the people in my life to remind me of His existence, every so often He would show up in a way that I couldn't avoid or deny. One of those times was during a particularly stressful move. Our kids were still little, and we were moving into a place that would better suit our growing family's needs. It wasn't a big move; it was just about a mile down the road from where we were living. But obedient to Murphy's Law, everything started to go sideways.

The sale of our house, which seemed like a done deal, suddenly sounded like it would fall through. Due to an oversight on our part, we had packed up our refrigerator to move to our new place. This was a no-no. We were supposed to leave the refrigerator, and the new owners were seriously displeased. It's one of those little things that feel much bigger and much more stressful in the moment than they do later.

I drove to the new house frustrated, tired, and aching from our move. As I drove, my back spasmed. It had already been hurting badly; but as I drove, each small dip in the road or vibration of the truck made the pain almost unbearable. I was in such agony, I did something uncharacteristic—I prayed. "God," I cried out, "if you're really real, You'll make my back stop hurting." To my shock, the pain in my back immediately stopped. Seconds later, I was filled with overwhelming fear. This answered prayer meant that God was real and He was near. It didn't change the fact that I didn't really want anything to do with Him, but it did shake my belief that He was not exactly the absentee landlord I thought He was.

When I arrived at our new home, I tracked down Kristin and told her the story. She listened with what I felt was a rude indifference. "Yeah, okay," she said when I had finished the account of my miraculous journey.

Yeah, okay? Her response was pretty anti-climactic. I had just conceded that not only did God exist, but He had also healed me when I asked Him to. I went from not even being able to sit up in my pick-up due to sharp shooting pains, to instantly having no pain, and Kristin didn't even sound impressed. Sure, she was tired, it had been a long and tiring day, and she had our two small children to attend to, but I had expected a little more excitement than that.

Within weeks the memory of the experience faded, and I was back to being the old Peter. I still didn't like religion, and I didn't want to go to church. I continued to live my life by *my* rules. God was put back in the box I had manufactured for

Him all those years ago. Yeah, He existed, but so what? What was that to me?

It's hard to imagine how God would have reached me if it were not for Kristin. No matter what I said about her faith or how I sometimes mistreated her, she never gave up on God or me. For a number of years our marriage struggled, and we became increasingly distant from one another.

Kristin turned to prayer to save our marriage. She didn't pray for God to change me, although I wouldn't have blamed her if she had; she prayed that God would show her how to love me. I know God answered that prayer. I can look back now and see that He really did save our marriage. Even as I think about this now, it still brings me to tears.

In May 2013, Angus Buchan was coming to Murfreesboro. I had never heard of the man before, but apparently, it was big news. He would be speaking at the Mighty Men's event at Murphy's Center at Middle Tennessee State University. Everywhere I went, people seemed to be talking about it. I stopped counting the number of invitations I received. I was an occasional churchgoer now, but the Mighty Men's event seemed like a whole new level of crazy Christian, and I didn't want to be one of them.

The event was being held on a Friday night; happily, it was a night where I was scheduled to coach my son's soccer practice, so I felt justified in blowing them off. Unfortunately, Kristin started bugging me to go too. I could get away from other people when they asked, I could make up some easy excuse for why it just wouldn't work for me, but Kristin was another matter. Kristin knew my schedule. She knew perfectly well that I could afford to miss, or even cancel, that Friday night soccer practice. It irritated me. "Listen, you know me. You know I'm not going to some Mighty Men's conference," I said to her.

Kristin didn't give up; she just shifted gears. Angus Buchan, the old, South African farmer turned Christian evangelist, would also be speaking at our church the following Sunday. Everything in me rebelled, but I was starting to get tired of fighting it. "Fine," I said. "But we're going to the 8:30 service."

Kristin nodded and I grinned. Kristin was notoriously late, even for the 10:30 service. There was no way she would be up and ready in time. I didn't like being late to things, so if we happened to be super late on Sunday morning, we would just end up going to Waffle House instead. It had happened before, and I was confident that is exactly what would happen that Sunday.

Early that week, I got a call on my cell phone from someone in the church. I had no idea how she got my number; I don't usually hand it out. She said that there was going to be a special meet and greet with Angus Buchan, and it would be great if I could attend.

I refused politely.

She insisted politely.

She was so good at being insistent without being pushy that I felt like I had to give an excuse. "I don't know what my calendar holds. If I'm free, I'll come. But if not...well, you understand if I won't be able to make it."

"Absolutely, we hope you will make it. It really would be wonderful to have you there." The conversation would have been a whole lot easier if she weren't so friendly and so extremely polite.

"I'll try, but I do have a meeting at work that morning,

but I'll come if it falls through for some reason." I was relieved that I remembered the meeting. It wasn't a big deal. I could have easily canceled it since it was just with a couple of my managers over a non-urgent matter. If I wanted to sleep in that morning, I probably would have blown it off, but she didn't need to know that. She hung up the phone thinking I was a kind and accommodating person. I hung up, happy in the knowledge that I didn't have to go.

That Thursday, financial statements for the restaurant came out, and they were at best grim. If the calculations were correct, and I doubted they were, it was saying that we'd had a considerable loss that month—the kind of loss that could close all five restaurants in two months if the numbers were correct. I called my sister who handled our books and asked, "These numbers can't be right, can they?" She agreed that something seemed off, but she had gone over them and as far as she could tell, those were the correct numbers.

I called the accountants in a panic, and they promised they would review it. "We can meet you on Monday morning to go over them if that works for you." I agreed. I hung up the phone and laughed out loud. I had thought I was making an excuse about a meeting on Monday morning, but now I legitimately couldn't make the meet and greet with Angus. In fact, I had to cancel my original Monday morning meeting as well.

Friday evening, I took my son to soccer practice. Only two other boys showed up, and they were from a Muslim family so would not be attending the Mighty Men's event with the rest of the members of the team. There wasn't much I could do with just three boys, but I didn't mind. I went to bed that night feeling pretty pleased with myself for avoiding the Bible thumpers conference.

That Sunday I went into work early. I had some things to sort out before the service, not that I really expected to go but it would be nice to take some time off with the family. To my surprise, Kristin met me at the restaurant with both kids dressed and ready to go EARLY! It was annoying.

Our church is big. It has thousands of parking spots. The parking lot is usually full by the time we get to church, but this time we were so early that the parking lot was practically empty. We dropped the kids off at the Children's ministry area and found our usual seats near an arched doorway at the side of the auditorium.

I used to call it the mouse hole, not because it was small but because the shape looked just like the kind of mouse holes in Tom and Jerry cartoons. I felt it offered an easy escape if the need arose.

I was surprised at how few people were at the service. With all the hype I'd been hearing, I expected a packed house. A guest musical group, Stikyard Percussion, took the stage. I wasn't upset about that. They were good—really good. Then Pastor Allan came out and explained that Angus Buchan would be speaking at the later service.

How awesome! I couldn't believe my luck; I didn't want to hear him anyway. I was thrilled. It's like when you are dreading an awkward social gathering, and then the host cancels. You feel immensely pleased with your good fortune as if you somehow willed it to happen.

Kristin, on the other hand, was not happy. She had really wanted to hear this guy, and because I forced her into going to the early service, she wouldn't be able to. She sat, arms and legs crossed, shoulders tense; I could feel angry waves emanating off of her.

We picked the kids up at the end of the service, and Kristin was still fuming. I decided to make things better by planning a fun, family day outing. I was sure that I could pull her out of her funk and get her to forget all about it.

As we exited the church, it was to swarms of people. They must have been there, lining up at the doors for at least half an hour already. It was weird; this wasn't a Black Friday Doorbusters Sale. Could all these people really be here to listen to an old crazy farmer talk about Jesus?

The crowds only affirmed for Kristin what she would be missing. It was a big event, and I had denied her the chance to go. As we headed to the car, she again began to insist we go back. She wanted to stay; it wasn't too late. There was no way I was going to sit through two services in one morning, so I said, "Okay, listen. I'll drop everyone at home, and then you can come back with the car."

It would ruin my plans for the family outing, but at least it should keep us from all-out war. We pulled out of our parking spot and headed for the exit. The line up of cars went right out onto the road. "Look! They're all going." Kristin pleaded her case. "If you hadn't insisted on the early service, we could have already been there and had good seats."

"Fine!" I said, "If you want to go so bad, I'll turn this car around and drop you off."

Now we were both angry. She insisted that's not what she wanted. She had wanted us to go together.

"Fine! I'll come." I was too frustrated and angry to do anything else.

Kristin looked at me and rolled her eyes, "Don't be a martyr."

Silence reigned for a moment, but I turned the car around

and headed back. Kristin studied my face, and with slightly less acid in her tone, she said, "We don't have time to drop the kids off anymore, anyway."

"Fine, they can sit through it with us." If I was going to suffer through it, so could they. So much for a family outing.

When we finally got back into the church it was packed—I mean sardines-in-a-tin-can packed. There were only a few hard plastic chairs off to the side still available, at an angle where you couldn't see anything that was happening on stage. You may as well have listened to the podcast later in the comfort of your own home. I was now the one sulking like a 42-year-old toddler. The chairs were uncomfortable. You couldn't see anything, and I had already sat through one whole service already in a place where I didn't want to be!

A friend of ours, named Terry, spotted us. "Peter, Hi! I've got some seats over there in the middle, they're yours if you want them." These would be the padded seats, much more comfortable. I wanted to be comfortable, yet the middle was far away from my mouse hole. This was a dilemma. I started to reject him politely, but Kristin spoke up again and took the seats.

The seats were smack dab in the middle of a group of guys, who looked like they could be former hells angels. They were all tatted up. My son Jamey was seated next to a big guy with a round face and curly hair. He smiled down at him and introduced himself. "I'm Ian," he said. "And I've flown all the way from England just to meet you."

Jamey's mouth dropped open a little at that. I was relieved that he seemed nice. We found out later that the group was made up of men from all over the world who travel with Angus to pray for him.

Stikyard came on stage just then, and I was happy about that at least. I enjoyed them just as much the second time. All too soon Pastor Allen had taken the stage and was introducing Angus Buchan. The much-lauded man appeared in blue jeans, flannel shirt, cowboy boots and hat, and carrying a huge Bible. He wasn't a big man, but he had a big presence. He started by saying he wanted people to be fired up for God like the Zulu warriors from the area of Africa where he lives.

He had everyone shout "Amen!" at the top of their lungs with a fantastic amount of enthusiasm. My son got into it very quickly, but I just thought it was like some spiritual pep rally. The whole church got into it, and once again I was regretting not sitting near my mouse hole.

Angus's message was all about how God uses ordinary people. He used biblical examples like the story of David and Goliath. David was the youngest in his family, still just a boy, and his brothers were grown men, soldiers fighting in battle. But it was the boy, empowered by God, who slew the giant.

He talked about how God chose Joseph, again one of the youngest in the family. He was the dreamer. God set him up in Egypt as second only to Pharaoh in power. Joseph was a foreigner, who not only pulled the nation of Egypt through a time of terrible drought but saved his own people as well.

God often shows up to the unlikeliest of people and makes His power known through them. He ended his examples with Jesus and shared how God Himself came in the unlikeliest form. When He came to save us from our sins, He put aside His omnipotence and spent nine months in a womb. He was born to parents who had weathered a scandal about His conception. He was born at a time and in a place and to a people that were under the control of a foreign power.

By human standards, Jesus was nothing special, less than that in fact. His family was in many ways substandard. And yet, at the same time, He is fully God. He did impossible, mind-blowing things as He walked the dusty roads of occupied Israel. And then, to top it all off, He died in a horrific way, in payment for our sins, only to beat death and rise from the dead three days later.

As Angus explained how God calls ordinary people to take part in His greatness, I felt a pull. He went on to say, "God has a plan for you. Will you choose it? Will you say yes to Him?"

He ended his message with an altar call. I don't exactly remember what words he used. I do remember getting to my feet. For the first time ever, I felt compelled to do something that I did not want to do. It wasn't that I lost control of myself; it was more like a sudden craving as if I had just finished eating something delicious, and I wanted to keep eating even though I was already completely satisfied. It was like something so good that I wanted more.

Kristin was beside me, and when I stood up to go to the front, I think she probably thought I was headed for the mouse hole. No one else around us was standing. I quietly explained to her that I wanted to get to the front. She looked at me like I was crazy but relented very quickly; she and the kids even went up with me, maneuvering past the big biker looking guys and making our way up onto the stage.

When we first started to make our way up, I remember thinking how awkward it would be up there. From the looks of it at first, there would only be about fifteen maybe twenty people up there with me. A song was playing as we took our place near Angus. By the end, the stage was packed. I would guess there had to be about two hundred people up there. On top of that, the whole church started to move into the aisles towards the front, supporting us in prayer.

I normally hate crowds, but I wanted to be there so badly it didn't matter that I was rubbing shoulders with strangers. I couldn't say why I wanted to be up there so much; I just did. When it seemed like everyone that wanted to come had come, Angus started praying for us. He prayed and he prayed. He kept praying for us all until well past noon.

When we finally left the church, I realized I was hungry. I'm generally very time oriented and always have my watch, but even without it, I could probably guess the time. But up there, on that stage, all measure of time had disappeared for me. It was later in the day.

I could hardly believe that I had spent an entire morning at church. Crazier still was that I had voluntarily gone to the front for prayer. I felt a little confused by what had happened to me. I didn't like the fact that I went. I couldn't explain why I answered that call when I had nothing to gain. It was kind of scary and uncomfortable. It made me want to hide away and think about what it all meant.

Kristin, on the other hand, was talking a mile a minute. She does that when she gets excited. As we drove home, she wanted to go over everything that had happened. Kristin wanted to dissect everything that Angus had said and what had compelled me to go up that morning. The more she talked, the more I withdrew.

I convinced myself the reason I felt compelled to answer the altar call was that Angus was such an unconventional and motivational speaker. I had felt like this before when my back got better. Everything will be back to normal within a couple of weeks, so surely this feeling would also disappear.

To block from my mind what had just happened, I turned my thoughts to my financial crisis; it needed my time and attention anyway. If the error in our records couldn't be found our restaurants could be in big trouble.

When I got to the office the next morning, I started preparing for my meeting when the accountants called to say they found the error, that it was an easy fix, and they wouldn't need to see me that morning after all. As happy as I was that we weren't on our way to bankruptcy, the cancellation of our meeting meant that my morning was suddenly wide open. I had committed to go to the meet and greet if I was free, and now I was. Grudgingly I went.

The meeting was held in one of the smaller sanctuaries in the church. It was set up with round tables and a breakfast buffet on the far side of the room. There had to be close to a hundred or so people milling around, making small talk and eager to meet with Angus Buchan.

I had been to meet and greets before, so I had some idea of what to expect, but it didn't mean that I wasn't awkward and uncomfortable. I tucked myself away at a side table with a cup of black coffee and studied the others there. I was so sick to my stomach that I had ended up at there, I couldn't even eat.

As I continued to people watch, I caught sight of Ian, the big English guy who had sat beside Jamey. I figured he was probably uncomfortable, not knowing anyone there either. I walked over, smiled a greeting, "Thanks for talking to my son. I have to tell you that after we were leaving, my son asked me, 'Is it true that man flew all the way from England to meet me?' He is a very gullible kid."

I laughed thinking I was sharing a cute story. Ian looked

at me straight-faced and said, "I did. I don't know why God placed me beside him, but I am sure that I was sitting beside him because God wanted me to be there and meet him."

Our talk only lasted a few minutes, five minutes at most; I didn't know what else to talk about, and I didn't want to stick to the topic of Jamey. It was like I was getting scolded for saying something stupid. I chuckled awkwardly and made my way back to my seat.

The sincerity in Ian was shocking. It wasn't until a couple of days later that I realized he really was telling the truth. God ordains meetings like this.

Angus came in just then, and I shook hands with him as he walked through the crowd. Angus took the stage to address the room. As he spoke, it was as if he were looking right at me, although I'm sure it was actually the Holy Spirit making me aware that he had something to say to me.

Angus asked this question, "Are you willing to die for your country?" I quickly made up my mind that I probably could, but it was his next question that pierced my heart. He asked, "Then why are you afraid to speak out for God?"

That question hit me hard, so hard that I can't remember anything else Angus said that morning. I can still hear those words of his clearly. In a fog, I left that meet and greet and got in my truck. Why am I so against speaking out for God? Why did I ever take offense to that? Why, if I believed He existed and had even experience miracles, did I set myself against others who openly loved God?

I started that momentous drive to Memphis, and the struggle began in earnest. You know what happened next. I had started a wrestling match with God, and there was no escaping it.

It was only after Jacob's struggle with God and submission to Him that he acknowledges God as his God. He made it personal. (See Genesis 32:22-30.) Although I had believed in God, it wasn't until I had fought with God and submitted to His authority that I saw him as my personal God.

FIVE

A Whole New World

This brings us back to the day of my "holy shower," the day I was washed clean in every sense. Everything that had been weighing me down, every thought and experience that had become a barrier to a relationship with Christ was stripped away.

I'm not sure if you know the feeling of taking off a backpack that you have been carrying for far longer than your body felt capable; but when you shrug out of it and can finally straighten up again, there is this feeling of weightlessness. That is what happened to me in the shower when God removed the weight of guilt and fear from my life; I literally felt physically lighter, as if gravity had released its grip on me.

I had never before experienced such extreme happiness. Everything around me seemed better: the air felt fresher, and my hotel room appeared to be brighter and larger than before. And to my surprise, I couldn't wait to be around people. I had just spent the last few days of the conference holed up in my room, avoiding contact with humanity; now I desperately wanted to have that contact.

I dressed quickly and headed for our final meeting, hugging old acquaintances, slapping them on the back, laughing at anything and everything resembling humor. No matter what people were talking about and how boring that meeting was, it couldn't destroy the joy and energy surging through me.

In the book of Acts 1:8, it says, "But you shall receive power when the Holy Spirit has come upon you; and you shall be witnesses to me in Jerusalem, and in all Judea and Samaria and to the end of the earth." I am sure I had probably heard that verse before, since I had been dragged to church for so many years, but it was only after I received the Holy Spirit for myself that it could make sense.

Not only did I feel different, but I started to become the kind of person I once disliked. I became a witness to the goodness and grace of God. I couldn't shut up about Him.

I made God four promises that day: I would pray; I would read my Bible daily; I would no longer cuss; I would no longer look at porn. I started to keep that promise right away by downloading a Bible app on my phone and doing some basic web research where I found some suggestions for non-believers on how to read the Bible. It suggested starting with two of the gospels, Mark and John, because they tell all about the life of Jesus and how His life affects our own. It seemed like an easy enough plan to follow, and I started right away.

I drove home that day completely alert, despite the fact that I still had only slept a total of four hours in the last three days. I didn't even mind driving the I-40 that day, I was completely absorbed in the wonder of what I was experiencing. There was so much love and joy in my heart that it practically ached.

I was always excited to see my wife and kids when I got home from a trip, but I knew today's reunion would be a little different. I could hardly wait to be around them. I wasn't so consumed with the desire to get back home that I couldn't enjoy that drive though.

I did what I had done on my way to Memphis—I listened to sermons. Only this time they made sense to me. They didn't leave me with questions; on the contrary, they all seemed so logical. As much as I struggled before with understanding, I now could accept and believe. The ideas I had previously held about the person of God now seemed ludicrous. I had misjudged His character entirely. I had assumed God's character resembled that of some of the Christians I had known, as flawed as they were.

I now came to realize that any goodness in the character of the Christians I had known, Kristin included, was a mere reflection of God's own goodness. I came to recognize that God had never been absent in my life. It was me who had chosen to ignore and revile Him.

I had been baptized as a baby, but I suddenly wanted to be baptized as an adult. I knew that such a desire must come from God because in the day or two I'd just spent reading the Bible, I did not understand why I had to be baptized—I just knew I had to. Besides, what sensible adult wants to get dipped in some water in front of a bunch of people and then climb out again? If there weren't something significant in that act, there would be no point.

I arrived home that evening and greeted my family with more joy and playfulness than they probably had seen in me for a long time. When Kristin and I had a little time to ourselves, I followed her out to our back porch. She sat down on our little porch swing and let her feet drag back and forth on the ground, as the swing rocked in a gentle rhythm.

I hadn't told her yet what exactly had happened to me in

Memphis. I wanted to, but it was all so fresh that I was still processing a lot of it. I did tell her that I surrendered my life to Jesus and that I wanted to get baptized. The swing stopped, and she looked at me with a crooked smile and mixture of excitement and disbelief. "Are you serious?"

I grinned, "Yeah."

I could tell from her face and her fifteen seconds of silence that I had managed to shock her. I knew I would shock her even more when I related some more of the details of my experience in Memphis. She was, as usual, full of questions. But she also sat in disbelief as I filled in more and more particulars.

She could tell, even before our conversation on the porch, that something had changed, but it was the real transformation in me that astounded her. She had gotten my texts while I was still away, the ones that were uncharacteristically sentimental and affectionate, but she had just thought I was being weird. And for me, I was. But I wasn't the old Peter anymore.

While in Memphis, I had mailed my pastor a letter that touched on what had happened to me and how grateful I was for his sermons. I thanked him for his role in my salvation. I knew he must be busy as the head pastor of an enormous church, but his assistant contacted me quickly and set up an appointment for the next week.

When the day came to meet with Pastor Allen, I was scared to death. In my mind, he embodied "the church." That included all those Christian kids that had once bullied me, all the Christian kids I had once bullied, the lady who had asked me not to come back to church, and the pastor who quit meeting for Bible study with me because I asked too many questions.

But the church also included Kristin, who had quietly and

consistently invited me to join her in faith. It included Angus Buchan and Ian, the English guy who had challenged me and encouraged me to get to know God in a way I hadn't before. And it was Pastor Allen himself, and all the sermons I had heard that had played a part in my surrender to Christ.

We met in a tiny conference room at the church. My heart was racing, and my hands were clammy as he sat down with me. I had a difficult time looking at him and was nervous every time he scratched something on his yellow legal pad. I explained again what had happened to me both in Memphis and over the course of the weekend at the church. Then I told him, "I'm really just here to thank you. I know you're a busy guy, and I don't want to keep you too long."

He shook his head with a smile, "With a letter like the one you sent, I figured we deserved to have a meeting. In fact, if you're willing, I'd like to meet with you once a month." It didn't take long for me to feel comfortable with this man. Even though he is one of the most intelligent people I know, he can talk on my level and frame his sentences in a such a way that I quickly felt at ease.

By the end, all the nerves had melted away, and we were able to have an excellent talk. Just before I left, Pastor Allen gave me a book his parents, the founders of our church in Murfreesboro, had written, called *An Extraordinary Life*. It talks about the "seeds of the extraordinary" that God provides each of us.

It seemed to fit perfectly with what God was revealing to me these short weeks. Every morning I would get up, pray, and read fifteen minutes to an hour from my Bible app. I had so much to learn, and my appetite for the things of God was voracious.

I left that meeting with Pastor Allen feeling drained. In just one hour, I had let go of a lot of hurts in my past caused by people who claimed to be children of God. It was a truce after a long-standing war.

All my negative experiences meeting with church leadership in the past could be cast aside. I had finally made peace with the church. It was as if I had just gone through an intense therapy session, and my memories had been healed. I left, no longer scared or nervous about meeting with Pastor Allen. In fact, I felt a real connection with him.

The drained feeling quickly left, and it was once again replaced with an energy and excitement that was a part of the new Peter. Pastor Allen had said to make sure we met again in a month, but I went in three weeks. I was so eager to have a chance to ask more questions and get to know this man of God better.

When I left the church that day, I went on the hunt for a real Bible. The Bible app was great, and it was super handy, but I like books. I think you see the words printed on paper differently. I wanted a Bible that didn't have too small of print, and something that was an accurate translation but easier to read than the King James Version.

I knew what I wanted, but I just didn't know where to find it. Tennessee is littered with LifeWay stores, I passed by them a thousand times, but I didn't actually know what they were. Instead, I found a little mom and pop publishing com- pany just down Broad Street in Murfreesboro. Many times before, I had driven by the little white building with "DeHoff Since 1939" written in big red letters on the sign out front, clearly stating that it was a Christian Bookstore and Publisher. I figured that if they didn't stock Bibles, they could probably at least tell me where I could buy one.

The little store did have Bibles, masses of them. They also had all sorts of church paraphernalia: offering plates, crosses, communions cups, marriage certificates; you name it, they probably sell it. It was a little overwhelming for a first timer. An older woman behind the counter by the name of Bonnie offered to help. She had eyes that smiled, and a face that shone with the reflection of Christ. She kindly talked me through some of the different Bible translations that they stocked. I was reading the New American Standard Bible on my app, but as I described what I was looking for she suggested I might prefer the New King James version.

I left with a sense of accomplishment. I had other Bibles at home, but they weren't just mine. I really loved that I could read from my very own Bible. I could make marks in it and write notes in the margins.

I soon knew where to find things in it. In my mind's eye, I could visualize just where a verse could be found on the page. My Bible is now very used and needs to be rebound; and although I could stop just about anywhere and grab a new one, I am sure I will take it back to the kind people at Dehoff's and have them fix it up for me.

The next big item on my Christian to-do list was my baptism. That summer our church was holding a Baptism Sunday. It wasn't too far into the future, so I signed up for it. Growing up in a Southern Baptist family, Kristin had a pretty good understanding about what baptism is, but I did not so I was happy to go to the baptism class that explained what it means for us as believers.

They said it was an outward expression of an inner change. It isn't membership into a denomination. It isn't a magical ritual that somehow marks you as a Christian so that you can enter heaven when you die. It is more like a marriage ceremony—a declaration before witnesses that you love God and you are giving yourself to Him.

Just like there are many ways people can hold wedding ceremonies, there are lots of legitimate ways to be baptized. Pastor Allen reminded us it didn't even matter where it happened, he had baptized people in barrels and hot tubs before. Some people are baptized in lakes and rivers, some in plastic kiddie pools. The important aspect of baptism was that it symbolized that I was dying to my old self and was now alive in Christ.

Before that class, I hadn't really thought about it as a public affair. I had thought it was actually very personal. And it is. But like a wedding, inviting people to witness this ceremony means you are asking them to play a part in this relationship. I was publicly giving my life over to God, and it was important that I asked the people I loved to witness that. Any casual observer, I thought, would have already seen the change in me.

But when I sent an email out, inviting friends and family to come to my baptism at World Outreach Church, it received a very different response than I'd expected. Friends would ask me to go for lunch, and at the end, with genuine concern, ask me if I was dying, and if I wasn't dying, why on earth was I getting baptized?

I am part of a workout group, a great group of guys, some believers and some not. But as soon as they got my email, they started the teasing. I couldn't be offended, even when the teasing felt mean-spirited. The truth was, I had already said many of the same things to the outspoken Christians in the group.

I was in that exact same place just a few months before. It was actually kind of funny to me that I was now on the receiving end. It seemed like appropriate payback, and I knew that if God could change me, He could also transform the men who were mocking my newfound faith.

My dad and sister were confused about why I was even getting baptized. I had been baptized as a baby, and in their minds, that should be good enough. I tried to explain that my baptism as an infant wasn't my choice. It wasn't an outward symbol of my desire to follow Christ; I didn't even understand who He was back then. I wasn't even able to speak; so how could I confess that Jesus was my Lord and Savior?

When the day of my baptism finally arrived, I was surprised by how many people from work came and more surprised by how few of my friends from outside work showed up. I remember teasing my friends later that if we were serving alcohol at the baptismal service, they would have been there with bells on; but the truth is, I thought they would at least show up because this was an important day for me.

All those who were getting baptized that day met together beforehand and were given purple shirts to wear. We were going to be dripping wet afterward, and the t-shirts not only showed people who in the crowds were getting baptized, but they ensured no one wore anything that might become a little too revealing once soaked with water.

They had two pools going, and two lines of people ready to go under. I walked into the pool. The pastor dunked me, and I walked out.

In all honesty, it was a little anticlimactic. I don't exactly know what I expected. I guess I was comparing the experience to when I was filled with the Holy Spirit in that hotel shower in Memphis. Although I wasn't being baptized for the experience, but rather as an act of obedience to God, I still felt a little let down that it didn't elicit some sort of profound emotion.

It was a good lesson for me. I needed to learn that our relationship with Christ cannot, or at least should not, be driven by our emotions. There are times when I will feel let down. There are days when I don't feel as in love with God as I have on other days. But no matter how I feel, God is still God. He loves me and I love Him. My role as a Christian isn't to seek out emotional experiences that help me feel closer to Him; it is to live in obedience to my Creator. Obedience is the most critical aspect of my walk with Christ. Jesus said, "If you love me you will obey my commands." That's what this baptism was about.

I was pleased that there were people whom I loved and held dear, that saw me live in that sort of obedience. I was glad that my son and daughter were there to see their dad offer his life over to the lordship of Christ. I had been talking to our kids more and more about God.

No matter how a conversation started, or what it was about, somehow God or His Word snuck in there. You'll have to ask my kids if this annoys them or not, but I can tell you that my kids were already well on their way to falling in love with Jesus before I even gave my life to Him.

I found that in the next weeks and months, my home life changed drastically and not just in what we talked about and how we spoke to one another. I found I wanted to do more and more things for Kristin. I tried to make her life easier. I wanted to do what was asked of me without complaint. I just desired to be a better husband in general. Oddly though, it felt like things were starting to change for the worse. She seemed to be getting increasingly angry with me.

It surprised me when I realized that it didn't hurt and offend me when she was mad, which is a significant change from old Peter. When Kristin got mad at me in the past, there was an immediate fear that she was going to leave me. I would tiptoe around her, trying my best not to offend. I would distance myself from her in order to avoid arguments. Now that fear was gone.

Although it may have outwardly looked like our marriage was worse off than it had been before, God was saving our marriage. Years earlier, Kristin and I had some significant marital problems, but we didn't fight because I was too afraid. Kristin and I probably fought more since I got saved than we had in our first fifteen years of marriage, but it was because there was a security in our marriage that we didn't have before. We know that Christ is in our marriage, and He is protecting it. It was actually healthier for us to fight and bicker like an old married couple than to tiptoe around issues as if we were merely colleagues worried about offending each other.

It turned out that Kristin's anger and frustration with me after I had given my life to Jesus had a lot to do with jealousy. Her anger wasn't directed at me personally—it was at the enormous change that had just happened. Although, on the one hand, she loved my transformation, it made her feel insecure and that I wasn't the same man she had married. We didn't have knock-down fights; they were just more frequent than before.

I remember one night in particular. We had come home from somewhere and were in our bedroom getting changed. I could see that she was angry. Her steps were short, and her every movement seemed to be executed with sharp precision. She finally burst out, "We can't go anywhere without you talking about the Bible and what you're learning in it."

"What's wrong with that?" I questioned.

That did not diffuse the situation. "I feel like Jesus is first, and I'm second with you."

"He is," I agreed.

Kristin knew that this was how it should be and that the healthy change in me was a result of this new mindset, but it didn't make it any easier for her. She was angry that I was suddenly putting God before her and the kids. She had become jealous of Him, and it would take a while for her to get over that.

Throughout much of the first part of my marriage, I was a good person to Kristin, but I was not a good husband. I provided for her, I didn't cheat on her, I never hit her—you know, all the things we husbands tend to pat ourselves on the back for. The truth is I was doing what I should have been doing except the most important thing—I was not there for her emotionally, and she knew it. I would sit in a chair in the same room and listen to her talk and talk about whatever was happening in her life, while I went into my own world in my head, "Peter Land."

But, worst of all, I would completely ignore her when she would get mad at me, and I was too scared to tell her if I was mad at her. The angrier I would get, the more I would shut down. This, of course, caused Kristin to get angrier as well. It was a cycle that we couldn't seem to break free from.

I have seen many marriages caught in this cycle of husbands and wives growing increasingly distant, both believing they are being the "bigger person" in the situation.

Kristin's prayers were the number one thing that helped to stop this unhealthy pattern of behavior, but I had to learn my role as well, which was perfectly defined in 1 Peter 3:7.

SIX

Kristin's Story

As wonderful as Peter is at telling his own story, I just want to offer my perspective as his wife, Kristin. I think that many times a person may seem drastically different in public, but it is when they are at home that you really see them as they are. The real test of a transformed heart is in the way they interact with the ones they love the most because those are the very same people that know which buttons to push to drive them up the wall.

While Peter was in Memphis, after the weekend services with Angus Buchan, I worried a little about him. He seemed stressed from work and kept texting me. He often messaged while he was away, but this time it was a lot more than usual, and the messages were really sweet. It seemed a little strange to me, definitely not the normal Peter, but to be honest, I didn't give it much attention. I didn't even ask him what was up, or why he was acting so strangely.

It wasn't long after he arrived home again that I noticed his eyes were different—they were brighter somehow. I could see that he seemed happy about something. I don't even know how to explain it, but he was so full of life and joy. Peter's eyes change color when he's happy, and I guess I chalked it up to his mood.

It was a few days before Peter told me what had happened

in the hotel room in Memphis. As he related the details of his experience to me, I didn't know what to think. I was a Christian, I had been most of my life, but I had never had an experience like that. It sounded weird. In fact, it made me feel a little uncomfortable. I had grown up in a house where we didn't talk about the Holy Spirit that much. It's not that we denied that part of God, we just weren't the types to go searching out those kinds of experiences. I couldn't deny that whatever had happened to Peter was profound and deeply spiritual, but I just didn't really know what to think about it, so it was hard for me to share in his excitement.

I was happy about the fact that Peter had given his life to Christ, but the immensity of what was happening in him didn't really register for me. I had never in my life seen anyone be so full of joy after turning their lives over to God. It may be because I hadn't really seen an adult come to faith before; in fact, not since high school had I seen anyone close to being a Christian. I had seen those teenage friends begin their walk with Jesus on a spiritual high, but slowly they had lost their initial joy and enthusiasm. I supposed that would happen to Peter too. Surely this change was temporary, just a phase that he would grow out of.

When Peter told me about his letter to Pastor Allen and said he was going to meet him, I again felt uncomfortable—why was he going to bother that man? Obviously, Pastor Allen was a busy man with lots on his plate.

"I have a lot of questions, and I really don't want to lose this feeling I have" was Peter's response.

I couldn't fault him for that. Who wouldn't want to be happy and joyful for the rest of their lives?

That first Sunday, after Peter had gotten home from

Memphis, he was a bundle of energy. He hurried us out of the house and into the car. He drove like a mad man. I mean, we were almost flying, he was so eager to get to church. I kept saying, "Calm down. They have a good thirty minutes of music; we won't miss anything."

He barely glanced over at me, he was so intent on what lay ahead. "No way," he said, "I don't want to miss anything, not even the music."

We didn't miss the music. We were there in plenty of time. It seemed like Peter was eating it up. He had his Bible app, and he was reading along. You could practically feel the concentration coming off of him in waves.

Over the next few weeks, I noticed another change. We weren't talking much about work, the kids, or our friends anymore. Instead, our conversations centered around the Bible and what Peter was reading. He had the Bible with him everywhere, and his voracious appetite for God's Word had also left him with a lot of questions.

When we talked about our beliefs before, it would practically end in a fight. But now the conversation was pleasant. When Peter would ask about a verse or story, he would listen with interest to my thoughts and opinions on it. It doesn't mean we never disagreed but gone was his animosity and the feeling that he was practicing one-upmanship. We could talk openly and honestly.

I liked that because of Peter's interest, I too was reading the Bible more and learning so much. Suddenly, the way we had talked before seemed inappropriate. I felt increasingly convicted about what we watched on TV and the language I often used. God was challenging me through Peter. I had been a Christian for the majority of my life, but in a matter of weeks, Peter was surpassing me in knowledge and understanding.

A close friend of ours ran into Peter at a grocery store and called me up afterward to ask what was going on. "He looked really different," she said, "not in a bad way, he just doesn't seem quite like himself."

"He does, doesn't he?" I nodded with the phone to my ear. "The truth is, Peter gave his life over to Christ a few weeks ago, and he's been acting weird ever since."

As much as I had wanted Peter to become a Christian, and as thrilled as I was that we could talk about faith without fighting, I was starting to get a little frustrated that *all* of our conversations were about the Bible, or church, or his talks with Pastor Allen. It didn't matter how they started, they always came back to that.

I was out with some girlfriends of mine, and we were talking about it. One of the girls assured me he would calm down in time, that I just needed to be patient. But another of the girls, whose husband had also recently given his life to the Lord and was transformed, totally got it. As we talked and I complained, I realized what my real problem was. I was jealous of Jesus. I used to be Peter's center, and I wasn't anymore. But my friend who was in the same boat told me off, "Oh honey, He's the one person you can't be jealous of."

But I couldn't help it. I couldn't help that my jaw would clench and my lips would form a straight line every time I wanted to vent about work or the kids and Peter would bring it all around to a verse or a devotional he had just read.

He wasn't just like this with me either. He was the same way at the restaurants. Slowly his faith infused everything he did at work. Many of our non-Christian employees believed, like I did, that it was a phase he was going through. A few of them, taking a page from Peter's book only a couple of months before, even said, "You can't talk about God at work. We could get sued."

Lucky for Peter there were a few strong Christians on staff that not only welcomed the change in their boss, but they also encouraged him to stand strong. They recognized what was happening in Peter was real and it would last. Peter's HR director, Amy, even researched how to go about incorporating faith into the workplace without breaking the law.

People who were skeptical about Peter's conversion in the beginning aren't skeptical anymore. Even if they personally don't believe in God, they can see that Peter is a new man. They can see it's real. And they know, if they have a conversation with Peter, it will eventually include something about God. He just can't help himself.

Being jealous of Jesus wasn't the only struggle I had with Peter's transformation. Christmas, several months later, was also a big debacle. First, I have to explain that usually Peter is the best gift giver in the world—it is his love language. His gifts are always big and elaborate. He pays attention to things you mention you like, and he incorporates those things into his gift. He is famous for his gifts. People would often ask what he had gotten me for a birthday, anniversary, or Christmas, and I would always be able to impress them with whatever it was. So I was rightly curious and excited that Christmas for what lay under the tree.

Peter handed me my gift in front of the whole family. It wasn't a large box wrapped in an oversized bow. It was small, and therefore more exciting. And then I opened it. My heart sank. It was a trip to Israel. I had wanted to go to Israel at some point but not now. Isn't a trip to the Holy Land something you do in your retirement? I don't remember seeing any brochures with young blondes rather than silver-haired seniors, popping up at churches. If he wanted to take the family somewhere, why not the Bahamas? Or Mexico. Or even Europe. I didn't even try to hide my disappointment.

Within a few hours, I was fuming mad. Who gives their wife a family trip to Israel for Christmas? Didn't he understand the risks associated with traveling to the Middle East? It was another one of those things he wanted to do because he had become a Jesus freak. He hadn't even consulted me before paying for it.

I didn't want the kids to know I was upset about it, but as soon as Peter and I were alone, I erupted. It resulted in an all-out fight that Christmas night. By the end, he had realized he pushed too far. He apologized, but it didn't change the fact that we were locked in.

Despite my anger, which I held on to for the duration of the time leading up to our trip, I still went to the info meetings and tried to get prepared. I decided to let go of my disappointment and get excited about it. So what, it wasn't a journey I would be making in my golden years, it could still turn out okay if we weren't all blown to smithereens.

Israel was completely different than I had expected. Along with the places I had heard about my whole life, there are big modern cities, beautiful beaches, and shopping centers. What really surprised me was how real touring various sites made the Bible seem.

By our second day there, God shook me to my core. I remember going to the bathroom and thinking over what we'd learned that day. I realized that again, God was intruding on my privacy. I remember saying to Him, "God, you can't even leave me alone for five minutes to go to the bathroom?" And then I realized He put me in this place at this time, and He wants me to know Him. He is pursuing me because He wants a relationship with me, not just a checklist of my "Christian deeds," such as going to church and reading my Bible.

It's interesting that both Peter and I had these profound experiences in hotel bathrooms, and both in places we didn't particularly want to be. There is a little water closet in Israel where God's Holy Spirit made a change in me. I realized that I had resented Peter taking over my role as the spiritual head of our family. I hadn't realized that I didn't trust Peter until all of a sudden, my lack of trust and my insecurity in him went away. I let go of all the control issues.

I loved the rest of our trip. I got over my jealousy of Jesus and could just stand in awe of the sacrifice He made for us. It was incredible to walk across the same land Jesus did, to look up at the same night sky, and to revel in the knowledge of His infinite love for us.

As we returned home, Peter and I settled into our roles within the family. As we did, I realized I had so much more respect for him as a person and a husband. I see now how the kids lean on him and how we learn from him.

If it wasn't for the transformation in Peter, I don't think my kids would have the relationship with the Lord they have now. The kids have someone modeling for them what it means to follow Jesus.

Our lives are entirely different as is the purpose of Peter's ambition now. We see the restaurants as a mission field. Instead of using the business to feed our own ego and line our pockets, we see it as a platform to do good. Sometimes this means that we will take heat for our convictions. People have a hard time hearing the truth. But we see how God is building us up and giving us strength.

Peter stands for God even if he is roasted and made fun of for it. I am a people pleaser by nature. It is a thorn in my flesh. But I try to follow Peter's example in this as he follows the example of Jesus. This means that we have lost a lot in the community. Some friends have quit calling. But this life we have now is one of purpose.

Because God got us on the same page when we were in Israel, I fell in love with Peter all over again. I love the new Peter—Peter the Christ follower. If that hadn't happened, I don't think we could have weathered the storms that came later.

I am not going to tell you we never argue or disagree anymore. We most certainly do. We are a normal married couple. But the difference is that before God did this work in our lives when we had problems, truthfully, we were probably looking for a way out. Now, that isn't even a thought.

Now we know we are together because God put us together, and we will be together until God takes one of us home. He has given us purpose as individuals but also as a couple. Despite trials and difficulties, we have a lot of joy in our marriage now. I understand in an entirely new way what it means to cleave to my husband and together to cleave to Christ.

Because of where God has placed us, we are exposed to all types of people. Peter has in many ways taken on a pastoral role in the restaurants, and I am so happy to support him as he leads people under our care to learn about Christ in a fuller way. It is exciting for me to see the way God is using Peter to help others find their way to Him.

Peter isn't a judgmental type. That means people are comfortable to talk with him about all sorts of things. Without judging them, he leads them toward truth, inviting them to lay their burdens down at the feet of Jesus. They feel loved by him. Because of this change in him, many of our general managers, also strong Christians, also take on this role. Peter and the general managers learn from each other, building each other up spiritually and that transfers to our staff.

It hit me the other day as I was praying, how thankful I am for our general managers. The restaurant industry usually is quite rough. Drinking, smoking, and cussing are the standard. But now, in our kitchens, if someone cusses, someone is going to say something. The environment is a lot healthier, and the employees actually thrive in it. "As iron sharpens iron" (Proverbs 27:17), they strengthen my walk with the Lord.

There is one last thing I want to add before I finish. I don't want you to think that because of one magical experience Peter has it all figured out and is living a perfect and sinless life. He still has things he has to deal with, and it's really neat to watch him battle it out and see him push through the hard times without using anger as his driving force.

Now he recognizes anger as a sin in his life. He doesn't try and justify it. He isn't self-righteous about it. He still fails sometimes. He isn't perfect, but he's working through it. Peter doesn't try and present himself as something he isn't; he will be the first to admit he fails and has flaws.

The real miracle of Peter's life isn't that all troubles and faults disappeared. They didn't. The real miracle is that Peter has given control of his life to God, so that when problems come and he fails, God raises him back up and puts him on the right path.

I am so thankful that I got to see the whole transformation. I know that because I witnessed this transformation in Peter, it transformed my walk with Christ. I have no words for how thankful I am for that.

SEVEN

Taming the Tongue

"No more cussing" was number three of the four promises I had made to God that momentous day in Memphis, and in fact, during those days and nights as I researched all sorts of things about Christian life. I specifically looked up, "Can you cuss as a Christian?" The truth was I didn't want to stop. I loved cussing. I used to cuss so much that I would add curses to the middle of words. I thought I was making a point or at least making my point stronger.

By keeping cuss words as a part of my vocabulary, I figured it would show that Christians were real people. I didn't want to become a Ned Flanders from the Simpsons type. My brain refused the thought of me walking down the street saying, "Hi diddly dee, neighbor!" or shouting out "cheese and crackers!" when I stubbed my toe.

I did know of some Christians that cussed and had still led others to the Lord, and I had almost convinced myself it should be okay when I came across these verses in Ephesians 4:29,

> Let no unwholesome word proceed from your mouth, but only such a word as is good for edification according to the need of the moment, so that it will give grace to those who hear.

And if that wasn't clear enough, Paul goes on to write in the next chapter that there must be no "filthiness, nor foolish talking, nor coarse jesting, which are not fitting, but rather giving of thanks" (Ephesians 5:4).

That was it. After many opinions from a variety of sources, these two verses convicted me. Never allow other's ideas to trump God's truth. I took that to mean that God didn't want me to cuss anymore, so for me, it would be wrong. Since that day, I have come to realize that cussing would make people question my sincerity. It could even become a stumbling block for some. I can't see any value in cussing anymore, apart from trying to fit in with those whom I probably shouldn't be trying to impress anyway.

Surprisingly, curse words quickly disappeared from my vocabulary. I probably swore a maximum of five times in the next few months, and every time I felt horrible about it and repented right away.

The second thing I became acutely aware of was that God knew what was in my mind. Keeping curse words from coming out of my mouth was relatively easy, but I wanted to stop thinking them as well. I prayed, "Lord, you know I want to honor You with my thoughts. Please help me not to even think of cussing."

And although this is still a battle today, I can see that God has been working to clean up my thought life. Where curse words used to pop into my mind at least five times a waking hour, now it probably only happens every three months or so. Every time I think it, I still have to repent and ask for forgiveness.

A few months later while I was watching a movie, there was so much swearing that I found it really bothered me.

Something about it made my skin crawl; I had to turn it off. It probably was a good movie, but I just didn't feel right watching it.

That's when I realized that God had changed this area in me, although this doesn't mean that I sit in judgment of others when they use coarse language. It rarely bothers me much if others I know swear unless it is as much as I used to. Purposefully filling my mind with those words I used to love feels like taking a bath in swamp water.

I didn't tell anyone I didn't want to cuss anymore. I just stopped, but people noticed. One day I had to confront one of our managers who had messed up. It was a significant mistake that needed to be corrected. I didn't just tell him off, I gave him a dressing down. I really let him have it. Later, when his general manager asked what had happened, he said, "Man, Peter really cussed me out." He was about to launch into a detailed account of our meeting when he fell silent. He thought for a minute and then said, "That's weird. Actually, he didn't. He didn't cuss at all."

Another day I was in the kitchen at one of our restaurants and overheard one of our managers, who isn't a Christian but used to swear like a sailor, telling one of the other employees not to cuss. "We are a Christian company; you don't need to use that kind of language around here." He was firm.

If you have seen any episodes of "Masterchef" or "Hell's Kitchen," you might realize that in the restaurant industry, eliminating swearing from people's vocabulary would be almost impossible. I became aware of a change recently at one of our locations. Filtering out from the kitchen was some R-rated language. I never said anything to them, but I wanted to. It turned out I needn't have worried. Their area supervisor, in a monthly update, told me they had noticed it too and were addressing the problem. My choice in honoring God by controlling my language is having a snowball effect on others through management.

We know that our actions and words reflect on those around us. If someone comes to work in a foul mood, the entire atmosphere can feel heavy; soon the whole restaurant is on edge. But the same is true when someone comes in with a skip in their step and a smile on their face. Their lighthearted energy starts to make others feel happier as well. We *can* change the atmosphere.

I am not a rah-rah type of person. I wasn't before I was saved, and I still am not. So, I don't mean that when you report to work, you should plaster a fake toothy grin on your face and tell everyone, "good job," whether you mean it or not. The little things we do are noticed by others, and the impact is exponential.

We don't always realize how patterns of behavior, negative or positive, over time will influence not just the atmosphere but the culture of a place. Our restaurant culture, which had been predominantly secular for twenty-three years, went through a change.

A little while ago we were shooting a video of employees for our website. We asked them to tell us why they chose to work for us. We were totally open to whatever they might want to say. All of the interviews were great; I loved listening to them. However, sadly my favorite one isn't useable. Something went wrong with the mic, and the sound didn't come through clearly.

Anthony has worked at Demos' restaurants for half his lifetime. His interview touched my heart so much it made me want to cry. Back when he started, Anthony was a fifteen-year-old kid with a baby face and closely-cropped curly hair, short on height but big on personality. He was hired along with his cousin who shortly afterward walked out of his job. His cousin ended up in jail, while Anthony stayed on with us. Being young and a little immature at times, Anthony kept getting himself into trouble, doing things that would earn him a demotion.

But he didn't quit. With time and effort, he rose back up, progressing through the ranks. Eventually, he became the kitchen manager of one of our restaurants. Again, his immaturity took hold, and he quit in a way that showed he meant it. He was burning his bridges.

But some bridges can be rebuilt. After a time, we hired Anthony back. His hard work, training skills, and common sense earned him the role of kitchen manager at our highest volume restaurant. Through the years, I have worked with Anthony, counseled him on personal problems (whether he wanted to hear it or not), and have yelled at and chastised him for a variety of reasons. Anthony probably knows me as a boss better than 95% of the people that worked for us.

Today, Anthony has grown into an amazing man; he still has a baby face and short curly hair, he never made it much passed five-foot-seven, and his personality is as large as it has ever been. But he is also one of the top managers in our company.

What you won't have a chance to see from his interview was his testimony of what changed in our restaurants in recent years. He didn't have to talk about it, but when he did, I was completely caught off guard by what I heard. He shared about when he first heard me speaking of bringing Christian values into the business. "At the time," he said, "I didn't believe it would last." He thought it was a phase, and frankly, he just did not believe me.

I couldn't believe what I was hearing. I have always considered myself a direct person; when I said something, it was probably going to happen. Here was a long-tenured employee saying that he thought it was going to be a phase! Really?

Fortunately, he continued by saying that over time he started to see the positive effect it was having on the business and was intrigued. The more he saw the change in me, the more he wanted to know what had happened and how he could be a part of this change. I never went to him and beat him over the head with a Bible, telling him how to live his life. I just started using real words, showing love for others by not cussing them out, and most importantly, explaining to people that my change was due to my relationship with Jesus Christ.

He attended one of our Bible studies, and then he kept coming. He started bringing his kids with him to church. After about a year of Bible study, he gave his life to the Lord and was baptized. He talks with people about Jesus, and he is invested in learning about God's Word. His life has become a positive influence on those around him. I have to laugh when I look back at where we both were at one time.

A critical component of Anthony's story is this: Having Jesus change me is one thing, but making certain that those around me knew the change was because of Him was vital. The manager, who remarked that I no longer use cuss words, used to tease me saying that I was going to be a pastor, but he still recognized the positive impact Jesus had on my life by helping me control my tongue.

What had been a personal conviction turned into a public witness of God's transforming work.

EIGHT

Using the Tongue

I hadn't shared with many people the story of what God had been doing in me, but word about Peter 2.0 was getting out. It happened partly because of the changes we were instituting in the restaurants, but in larger part, because I really was a changed man. I received a call a few months after I had started to open up with friends and co-workers about my new-found faith. The person on the other end of the phone told me they were from a group called Living Sent Ministries, a collective of Christian business owners. "We would love it if you would come and share your story at our annual banquet," they said.

I have no idea how the group got my name or why they wanted me to speak. I had shared my story with handfuls of people but never to a group of more than five or six. This was to be a banquet with around one hundred and fifty attendees. As I stuttered through some questions, the most significant being, "Why me?" they explained that they had lined up a Christian executive to come and speak, but when a terrible storm had forced them to reschedule, the executive was not available for the new date.

I was intimidated at the thought; you'll remember that I was never someone who wanted to be behind a microphone. But the strangeness of the situation and my experience thus far of the way God works, made me think that this invitation was orchestrated by Him. If my mouth was the Lord's, I shouldn't just be worrying about what I don't say, I should also care about what God might want me to share.

If He wanted me to speak, I would. I may shake the entire time, my knees might feel like jelly and my teeth might chatter, I might get off the stage and run to the next room to throw up in the garbage can like I did all those years before, but I needed to accept this invitation. I would be open to letting God use me this way.

I tried to sit down and write out what I would say. I wanted to be prepared. The odd thing was, every time I sat down to prepare my speech, something catastrophic would happen. I was regularly being called away. As the day grew closer, Kristin grew frustrated. "Honey, y'all just got to get something down on paper. It's not right to just show up unprepared."

She was right. I decided to lock myself away for a day and not re-enter normal life until I had something written down. I had no idea what I was doing really. I had no idea where to begin. But by the end of the day, I managed to have some notes written down.

The banquet hall was full. There was no storm to keep the masses home this time. I walked up to the podium, arranged my pages neatly in front of me, and stared out at that sea of faces. One hundred and fifty pairs of eyes stared back at me. It was intimidating.

But a funny thing happened as I started talking. God led me to share things that I hadn't written down and taught me a valuable lesson. I didn't even glance at the notes I had prepared. Obviously, God didn't want me to use my words—He wanted to use my mouth for His message.

Not only did that talk go better than I had expected, it also led to another speaking engagement a short time later. This time, the call came from the Christian Chamber of Commerce. Again, it was a large group, but this time I found I was less nervous than I had been at the Living Sent Ministries banquet.

I was telling my story, and just as I was getting to the climax, the fire alarm went off. I paused. I wasn't sure what I was supposed to do in this situation. Since I was behind the microphone, was I expected to take charge? I looked over at the organizers; they looked back at me without so much as a flinch. I looked at the audience, not a single person was moving. No one was rushing to the exit doors. There was no mad scramble to turn it off. It was deafening, but if no one was doing anything about it, who was I to make a fuss?

Finally, after some time had passed, Kevin, one of the organizers, came over to me, looked me in the eyes, and yelled into my ear, "Do you think you can go on with this?"

I nodded and walked back to the podium, I smiled down at the members of the Christian Chamber of Commerce. "Well, it isn't the first time the devil overplayed his hand," I said. They laughed, and I continued my talk. Within seconds the fire alarm stopped. It was like the devil himself realized the piercing noise wasn't going to stop what was happening there and gave up.

Since then, I have been invited to speak many times at various Christian events, and at almost every event technology will glitch at a crucial moment. And every time I find that God says what He wants to say, and even faulty laptops, or speakers, or microphones can't stop it.

I don't actually mind the technical difficulties. If any-thing, I feel like it's an indicator that God is going to do something great, and the devil is trying his level best to stop it like a child who throws a fit because they lost a game. It won't change the score.

God wasn't just teaching me to share about His work in my life to crowds of Christian businessmen and women. He was inspiring me to share His Word at work. I don't mean that I was quoting John 3:16 to everyone at the office or wearing Jesus Freak t-shirts. It was maybe a little more subtle than that but not by much. I am a firm believer that our actions reflect our words.

There is an accountability factor that comes in to play when we speak out. I recognize that I can destroy my credibility by hypocrisy. If God calls me to speak, I need to speak but I must also back my words up by my actions. My business decisions must be in tune with my faith. I will be under scrutiny because of my boldness.

I have been criticized by Christians and non-Christians alike for speaking out. They say I'm dumb because I could potentially lose much business by being overtly Christian. My response is that the Bible talks about a time when it will be hard for Christians to buy or sell or trade, solely because of their faith. If we can't risk 10% of our business now, how will we be able to risk 100% when the time comes?

If we pay attention to the news, we can already see society heading in that direction. If we want to stand strong in the future and if we want our children to choose Christ even when they might be labeled outcasts for it, then shouldn't we train ourselves for that possibility?

I've always loved stories, they are a fantastic way to

teach. When I spoke with employees in the past, I often quoted Thomas Edison or Albert Einstein and borrowed stories from our history books to give examples of what to do in certain situations. When I started reading the Bible for myself, I found that the stories in God's Word seemed so much more applicable than any I had heard or used before.

I was on a conference call with our general managers one day and noticed that many of them sounded worn out. It was clear to me that instead of delegating, they were trying to do everything themselves. I couldn't help but share with them the story of Moses and his father-in-law Jethro.

"Moses was leading a nation through some challenging times. The people of Israel looked up to him as a ruler and judge. Day and night they went to him to settle disputes, and Moses was wearing down," I explained.

Then I read Exodus 18:13-25. The story is pretty clear; with wisdom that comes from God, Jethro suggested a way for Moses to delegate authority to other judges, taking only the most difficult cases to pass judgment on. It was a solution that set in place our own system for settling disputes. By micromanaging, my managers would burn out. They needed to delegate. It wouldn't remove the need for their positions; it would free them up to do their job well.

When I asked who knew who Moses was, only three of the twelve people there raised their hands. I thought that since many of our managers and employees would have been school age when the movie, Prince of Egypt, came out, they would at least know the story of Moses. But most of them had no idea who he was or what he had done.

This had to change. It was a challenge. God was calling me to share more openly and deeply about this hope that I had in Jesus and the guidance He offers in His word. I can't tell you how many times I have been struggling through something and finally turn to the Bible for help and find the perfect instruction right there in my daily devotions.

The fact that so few people of my acquaintance knew the heroes of the Bible was a reminder that there are still so many people that don't have a relationship with our heavenly Father.

You may have heard of Penn Jillette, famous for being one half of the magic duo Penn and Teller. He is well known not just for performing some incredible illusions but also for his atheism. Although he does not believe in God, he famously said this about Christians who don't share their faith:

> I've always said that I don't respect people who don't proselytize. I don't respect that at all. If you believe that there's a heaven and a hell, and people could be going to hell or not getting eternal life, or whatever, and you think that it's not really worth telling them this because it would make it socially awkward—and to atheists who think people shouldn't proselytize and who say just leave me alone and keep your religion to yourself—how much do you have to hate somebody not to proselytize? How much do you have to hate somebody to believe everlasting life is possible and not tell them that?

> …I mean, if I believed, beyond the shadow of a doubt, that a truck was coming at you, and you didn't believe that truck was bearing down on you, there is a certain point where I tackle you. And this is more important than that.

You can find the video of Penn sharing this on YouTube. It's a vlog he recorded to tell the story of a man who came to him after one of his shows to give him a little Gideon New

Testament and Psalms. He was so touched by what this man did that he felt the need to share the experience with his fans.

I believe that churches have a fundamental problem, they are always inviting people to come and see, instead of going and telling. I admit that I was not particularly open to people sharing their faith with me when I was still an unbeliever, but I can tell you that it made an impact on me. Each person who attempted to introduce me to Christ shares a part in my testimony.

If we aren't looking for the harvest that Jesus talked about, we will miss daily opportunities to share the gospel. There are always people going through hard times; you don't have to look too far or long to find someone that is hurting. It is often the hard times that provide an opening to point someone to Christ.

Sharing my faith wasn't something that came easily. I remember that the first time I tried sharing my faith with a stranger was at a convenience store. There was a guy there grumbling to his friend about his troubles; amongst other things, his truck wasn't working, and it was going to cost way too much to fix. As I eavesdropped, I just felt this push to talk to him. I met him at the counter when he went to pay, and I just said, "God sometimes lets us go through these struggles. It gives us an opportunity to trust God through it and be thankful."

The guy looked at his buddy, and they both looked me up and down as if I had grown an extra arm out of my forehead as I spoke. That was it. We left and went our separate ways.

That may sound like a failed attempt to you, but I would disagree. I know that I was being faithful to the gospel. We have this obligation to tell people the good news. They are often blind to what God is doing. By simply mentioning His name and turning their minds to Him, even if only for a few seconds, it has the potential to affect change.

However, I think the real key in sharing the hope we have in Christ is when we ask Him to lead us to the harvest. If it's plentiful and if He's looking for workers, then we should ask the Lord of the harvest to lead us to the right field. In church speak, this is often called "divine appointments."

I experienced one of those a little while back. A remarkable example of God's timing, it seemed a lot like an inconvenience at the time. I had a meeting scheduled at one of our restaurants for 9:30 am and another at 10:30 am. Outside of those meetings I was going to spend the day at the office doing some catching up on admin work.

The fact that I had these two meetings pressing in on my already busy day made me a little frustrated, but when the person I was supposed to meet at 10:30 called to say they would be late and could we "push it back to 11:30," I was downright irritated. That would mean I would be stuck in limbo for an hour. I wouldn't have time to go to the office to work on the admin stuff, and I had no real reason to be at the restaurant.

I pushed down my indignation and decided to walk around and talk with the employees while I waited. Who doesn't love their boss poking their head in unannounced, right? As I made my way through the restaurant, I came across the wife of one of our employees. I remembered her well. Her husband had been going through some health issues, and we had been able to help them out. As a thank you, she had given me the gift of a journal.

You know how it is when someone you don't know well

gives you a gift, and it doesn't suit you at all, but you feel you have to gush over it a bit to make them feel good? That wasn't the case here. I actually really enjoy journaling. I used that journal she gave me all the time, jotting down thoughts that come to me in my devotions and Bible reading. One of the other minor irritations that day, was a result of misplacing the journal she had given me. Instead, I had been stuck painstakingly taking notes on my phone.

As I passed by the woman, I noticed that she was writing in a massive journal, easily the size of a ledger. I would have stopped to ask her about her seriously intense journaling, but she had headphones on and seemed not to notice me. I made a few laps talking with people, and when I came around again, I saw that her headphones were off.

"I've never seen a journal that big before," I said, stopping at the edge of her table.

She smiled, "I draw and write." She angled the journal towards me so I could have a look. It was pretty cool.

"I'm grateful for the journal you gave me; I use it all the time."

She looked pleased and asked, "What do you journal?"

My heart pumped just a little harder. I didn't know her well. I had no idea how she would respond, but since she asked, I was going to tell her.

"I use it for writing down thoughts and impressions when I'm reading my bible. If I feel God is teaching me something I shouldn't forget, it goes in the journal."

She nodded thoughtfully, "I'm not really into that religious stuff."

She must have noticed my eyebrows raise in question because she went on, "I've tried it. In fact, I've tried pretty much everything. I've bowed down to Allah. I've tried Buddhism, but it doesn't seem to work."

Some people might take this as a closed door, but it isn't—this is an opening! I told her, "For me, talking to God is where I get a lot of my wisdom for living."

She observed me with a look of curiosity. I was still standing beside the table, and if this conversation was being led by God it might take a little while, so I asked her, "Do you mind if I sit?"

She gestured for me to take a seat and I slid onto the chair across from her.

"It sounds to me," I continued, "like you are chasing answers. But to me the answer is simple, Jesus tells us to ask. Ask Him to reveal Himself to you. Ask Him to show you what is true."

She threw out a few more of her objections, and they were nothing I hadn't heard or thought of before. When I shared with her some of my story, she leaned in. God was doing something.

At one point, I grabbed one of the Bibles out of the lobby and showed her some of the verses that talked about how much God loved her and was waiting for her. And then, right there, between my first and second meeting of the day, I ended up leading her through one of the most awkward sinner's prayers on record.

Obviously, the Holy Spirit was at work. Despite my stumbling and nervous stuttering, God had touched her heart. She was bawling at the table, wiping her eyes with a napkin. I knew the feeling because I had experienced it myself. She was repenting and finding peace with God.

Just as we finished talking and I got up, I saw that my

11:30 meeting was just sitting down at the table behind me. I shook my head in wonder. It was obviously God who had moved the timing. The irritations—losing my journal and having that meeting pushed back—were actually set up by God. He had put all these things in place to make this divine appointment happen.

Kristin laughs about how changed I am. Now, if I go up to a counter at the grocery store and ask the cashier how they're doing that day, and they tell me they're having a tough time, I am going to share with them about Jesus. These one-on-one interactions allow people to see Christ in a new way. I've found that people usually feel better after our conversations and the times I prayed for them.

However, I still need work at knowing how to share the Gospel. I was just in Las Vegas last week, a place I hadn't been for years. The last time I was there, I wasn't a believer, and I obviously saw it with different eyes. This time, I was very aware of the hundreds and thousands of broken people living in this city. Of course, you will find these people everywhere you go, but as you are probably aware, everything is a little more overt in Vegas.

My first morning there, after my quiet time with God, I went for a walk. As I was waiting for the light to change, three young, scantily clad women were waiting for me, and one of them started asking me questions about what I was doing in town and how long I would be there. When she asked where I was walking, my senses began firing, I tried to read her face, wondering why she was being so nosey. Then, she asked if I would like to walk back to my room.

That is when I realized that these were three prostitutes leaving the hotel. I stuttered through my shock, "You don't

need to know my room number. I'm quite okay on my own."
I was so astonished that she would try to pick me up, but afterward, I was more upset that I hadn't taken the opportunity to tell her about the One who loved her enough to die for her.

Remember, success isn't in winning someone for Jesus. Success is overcoming any fear and inhibitions and sharing Jesus with those who need Him. It is the fear of speaking out that leads us to sin. The sin of silence is a sin of omission, and it's probably one of the most prevalent amongst Christians today. No wonder God charges us so many times to not fear.

Just because you fail to share your faith, doesn't mean you don't have the ability or the responsibility to share at the next opportunity. I had failed my mission in the elevator, but God gave me another chance at a Blackjack table with a woman who was the dealer. With no one else at the table, the conversation was easy to lead, and she revealed that she was at a crisis point in her life. I had a chance to share with her how Christ could help her through it.

As we learn from Ephesians, taming the tongue isn't just about what we don't say, it is also about training it to say what is right and good and true. We need to be intentional. We must train the tongue when to speak as well as when to be silent, trusting God to tell us what to say.

NINE

My Managing Director

One of the things I have learned about God is He sometimes creates complicated plot lines for our life stories that involve multiple players all moving toward a particular moment in time to bring about a big change in our lives. Like a master chess player with billions of chess pieces, He probably does this all the time. Occasionally, we get to see it, and when that happens, it's impossible not to sit back amazed in awe of His power.

After Angus Buchan's visit to Murfreesboro, I had kept in touch with the big, barrel-chested Englishman from his prayer team, Ian. We had exchanged emails back and forth, and I had told him all about what God had been doing in my life.

I loved the advice that I received from this man of God. It was a friendship worth cultivating, so when I heard he would be traveling back through Murfreesboro in a few weeks with Angus, I jumped at the chance to invite him for a coffee.

Days before Ian was set to arrive, I found myself in a meeting with a representative from Coca-Cola Consolidated. I am not sure exactly how we got to talking about God, except that it was tough for me not to. But since we were on the subject, the woman from Coca-Cola showed me the back of her business card.

Right there, carried with her wherever she went, was a purpose statement that read, "To honor God in all we do." I was curious about how a company their size would have a purpose statement that many would find politically incorrect. They are the largest bottler in the Coca-Cola family and have thousands of employees. How did they manage to keep God central in their purpose?

It has a lot to do with their CEO Frank Harrison, great-grandson of the founder, JB Harrison. Frank started at the company in the late 1970s. The environment wasn't a healthy one. My understanding was that it was a party place, and they weren't hiring secretaries for their skills. Frank wanted to do something about that.

He wanted to bring God into the equation, and to do that, the purpose of their business needed to change. A quick visit to their company's website will reveal that he has been successful in keeping God-focused, and he teaches others how to do so as well. I wanted that for Demos' and Peter D's, but I knew it would be a bold move. I was sure to get kickback.

I was still thinking about that meeting when I picked up Ian from the Embassy Suites Hotel here in town. He was waiting for me as I pulled up to the entrance, a gigantic grin on his face. I remembered him to be a jovial guy, but he seemed so genuinely happy to see me that I felt a little humbled. He took one look at me and said, "Wow, your eyes have really changed! They used to be so dark. I can see the change in you."

I'm not going to lie, that made me feel good and a little embarrassed, kind of like I was a little kid again being complimented by an adult.

Then he asked, "What's going on with you?" in his thick, Northern English accent.

"Not
much."

I gave the pat response that everyone expects. Only Ian wasn't satisfied with it.

"I think a whole lot has been happening with you." His broad shoulders were turned toward me, and his head was leaning close, waiting for me to really get into everything that had happened since I had said goodbye to him at that breakfast meeting in May.

I pointed out that the newly framed Peter D's was located between the hotel and the coffee shop and told him how it was all taking shape. We had one of the best teams, with over a hundred years of restaurant experience among us. He grinned and nodded, prompting me to wax a little poetic over it all until we got to the coffee shop and had sat down across from each other.

"So...with the restaurant. Who is your managing director?"

I was caught a little off guard by the question. I wasn't sure how that translated to American. Did he mean CEO? "Well...I am," I said, a little hesitation in my voice.

He shook his head. "No. God is."

"Well...of...of course. I mean, in that case, yes."

I felt a little awkward. I had totally misread that one.

"No," he said again. "In all cases."

I nodded, but he continued, "In all things. God is the one you turn to, to direct your path by giving control to God." He quoted Proverbs 3:5 (ESV), "Trust in the Lord with all your might and do not lean on your own understanding."

Although I understood this, I had to wonder about the practical aspect of how God can be the CEO. I tried to process what it was that God was asking me to do.

Our meeting was too short for my liking. All too soon we were standing to leave. Ian pulled out a couple of union jack beanies for my kids, and I drove him back to the hotel.

His question haunted me through those beginning stages of my faith. What does it mean for God to be your managing Director? I thought back to Coca-Cola's purpose statement and concluded two things: we had to honor God in all we do, and we had to look to Him for answers within the business. God was the real boss, and we were working for Him. I think that is the vast difference between a Christian running a business and a business that has been turned over to God.

I have read many books on managing a business, and all of them have relatively the same take: "You are 100% in control. You are the boss. You are the curator of your success." They tell you that to empower a team, it is you as the boss who is bestowing power on your employees to be successful in their positions.

If this is true, my business will always be on the edge of failure. Even now I make mistakes, trying to solve issues by my own wisdom before going to God for help. It is so much better to go to God first. When God is the managing director, the power lies with Him.

I decided to talk it all over with my assistant, Jennifer. Jennifer is a gift from God. I mean that literally. When I interviewed Jennifer for the job a few years earlier, she had no experience. The only reason I had even called her in for the interview was that multiple friends of ours had told me I needed to hire her.

They were right; I knew almost immediately that she would be a good fit. Jennifer wasn't so sure. "Are you a Christian? I will only work for a Christian," she told me.

I was shocked and a little offended by the question. Wasn't I the one giving Jennifer an opportunity in a position she wasn't actually qualified for? But the truth was, I did want her working for me, even if she was a Christian.

"Sure. Yes. But, I like to worship in my own ways." I lied, assuring myself that going to church was enough to make me basically a Christian.

When I did actually come to faith and told Jennifer about the experience, she was literally jumping up and down with excitement. It brought a whole new dynamic to our working relationship. On occasions that I hesitated about being too radical, she would encourage me to be even more so.

I told her I wanted to change our purpose statement from, "To take care of the total dining experience of a customer" to "Glorifying God by serving others. Serve and care for our customers and maintain accountability." She prayed about it too and encouraged me to share it with our managers at the next general meeting.

I had taken one of our manuals and changed the purpose statement on the front cover to the new one so that my managers could see it as an employee would see it.

I was excited and a little nervous as the meeting started. Our general meetings are usually boisterous. No one has any qualms about voicing their opinions. There was always loud discussion and the occasional disagreement, but we all really enjoyed each other.

I had pinpointed a few people before the meeting that I had expected to challenge me, but many of the managers already attended one of our work Bible studies, so I assumed that me talking more about God would come as no surprise. I handed the copies of the new manuals around the oval conference table, and the room fell silent.

No one spoke. No one even looked at me. All eyes stared straight down on the table in front of them, giving me an excellent view of the top of their heads. I asked them their thoughts. It remained quiet, very uncomfortably quiet.

After a few minutes of silence, I sat back in my chair with my hands behind my head and said, "I need to know what you think. You need to determine if I am completely crazy. You guys are the ones that are going to have to defend this to our employees."

I hoped I looked more confident than I was feeling at that moment. I was actually feeling very alone. I worried they might all walk out on me.

I looked around the table, hoping to make eye contact with someone and guilt them into talking. One of our new guys, whose big shaved head was the only thing I saw for minutes, made the mistake of looking up just as my gaze swept past him. His eyes quickly locked with mine, and he did a stellar impression of a goldfish with his mouth opening and closing repeatedly, and then he quickly showed me the stubble on top of his head again.

I pointed right at him, "You!" I exclaimed. "Go ahead! Say what you were going to say."

Poor guy. It came out like a command, but inwardly I was pleading. Timidly he voiced a concern. I don't even remember what exactly he said, but it opened the floodgates. Soon everyone was talking, albeit timidly. I had guessed correctly that the biggest issue for the managers was dealing with employees who could challenge them on these things. One of the managers, obviously a little fed up with the complaining, spoke up, "I don't know what the big deal is... aren't you all Christians?"

It was enough to bring out some explosive tempers. In seconds, it became a shouting match. It got so bad I had to call a break. Some people needed to breathe, including me.

When we reassembled, things settled down a little, and we managed to wrap it up. I realized something important that day—my managers hadn't had the same experience that I had. Instituting change was going to be a slow process. I needed to take every chance I could to introduce something to the group through teaching moments.

We started praying before meetings, and I made certain my Bible was visible for all to see. Slowly, I brought up our values and quizzed the managers on their opinions, "Would a non-Christian not want to work for a company that did not have the value of integrity?"

As I listened to their ideas surrounding our purpose statement and values, I was highly encouraged.

Listening to the managers in future meetings, I realized that the majority of the people that worked for us didn't understand what the values meant or even what values were. They might understand the word "dedication" but had never thought about what it means to them; they couldn't understand how to incorporate the value of dedication into our business.

We decided that in order for the values to have any actual value, we needed to teach them to the employees. We reworked our training guides, and I personally went to each restaurant to meet with each manager and teach them how to train the values.

It worked. In fact, one of our managers came up with the idea to teach a "value of the week," at every pre-shift meeting. It caught on with managers at other locations as well and has become something we do at all our restaurants. In fact, the managers developed an order and calendar for teaching so that we would be consistent across all our locations.

There was another notable change we made that was inspired by my meeting with the rep from Coca-Cola Consolidated. As she talked about ways they honor God, she kept referencing their chaplain service. She mentioned it multiple times, but I did not want to stop her and ask what she meant. As soon as she was gone, I googled it and found CCA (Corporate Chaplains of America), which turned out to be the same company Coca-Cola Consolidated used.

A chaplain goes to the business two times a week and just talks to the employees. They are not going in dressed in long black robes, hitting employees over the head with the Bible. They are there doing what Jesus commands all of us to do, loving people. If we did this, we could have a chaplain on call, 24 hours a day, 7 days a week, serving and caring for our employees.

The restaurant industry generally has many employees and a low net income. At the time, we had about five hundred employees so the expense would be significant. There wasn't a lot of encouragement from management for the program.

"That's crazy," I was told. "Have you even considered the cost? How do we even know the employees would use the service?"

The thing was that as much as I respected their opinions, I knew sometimes God asks us to do things that seem like foolishness by the world's standards. I really felt this was a God-inspired idea. I decided to go ahead and take my lumps later if I was wrong.

I was so glad I did. I can't even begin to tell you how valuable it has been in caring for our employees. The chaplains have made hospital visits, counseled and prayed for our employees, and provided marriage counseling.

I had assumed the biggest issue we would have is that our employees would laugh and blow them off. And to be honest, some did and still do. But I found that many employees and their families began to use and appreciate the program, calling on our chaplains for all sorts of issues.

One of the chaplains came to me one day and asked if I had met an employee in Nashville named Shawn. He told me, "That man has the joy of the Lord all over him. He is making an enormous difference there. You have to meet him."

It was an invaluable reference. I definitely wanted to meet this guy, but somehow, despite my best efforts, I kept missing him every time I was in Nashville. He would be off for the day, or just finished his shift, or he would arrive just after I left. I would have almost thought we were not meant to meet. But, low and behold, he transferred to our Murfreesboro location a short time later, and we noticed a change in that store as well.

The chaplain was right. He doesn't just have the Holy Spirit in him, he has the Holy Spirit pouring out of him in a flood. When I met Shawn, he wasn't exactly what I had expected. He was an ex-con, an ex-gang member, and there were some physical reminders of his past life. But there was such a joy and peace about him that also manifested physically. His smile was warm and inviting. His eyes had the spark and fire of life. The transformation in him was so complete it was hard to imagine he had ever come from that life.

But despite the joy and kindness that Shawn exuded, he

still had struggles. I hadn't known him long when I found out that he had an upcoming court date to deal with some parole fees incurred when he was moved from the severe crime list to the moderate crime list and had to be transferred from one parole officer to another.

I am not currently practicing law, but I still have my law degree, and so I decided to go with him. I just wanted to be there for him in case he needed any legal advice. I brought my Bible along, in case we needed to turn to it for encouragement or wisdom. But before I even cracked the cover, the court clerk took one look at it and said, "Don't you dare open that book in here."

"That Book?" THAT BOOK? The Holy Word of God? The only book where the Author comes along to explain His words! I felt the hairs stand up on the back of my neck. He had raised my ire. The only reason I held my tongue was because I didn't want to get Shawn in trouble.

Shawn, however, seemed untroubled. He smiled at me and as the guy walked away said, "We don't even need to open it. We have it in our hearts."

He was right. I believed that, but for just a moment I had felt like a victim of spiritual persecution. I had forgotten that because of Christ, we are more than conquerors.

I gained even more appreciation for Shawn that day. That shared experience outside the doors of our restaurants created a bond. We were brothers in Christ. I noticed Shawn treated everyone as beloved children of God. If they didn't know Jesus yet, he made sure they had a chance to get to know him; he never held back. And people responded to him. It was amazing.

As business owners, you tend to think that everything you

have to say is valuable and that all your employees are listening closely and want to hear what you have to say. It is the ego that gets in the way. The truth is, they often learn from and listen better to peers.

Shawn could get the message out in a way that the managers and I couldn't. He could talk about Jesus; he could share Christ's values, not as if it were a new policy being brought in, but as a testament to God's work in his life. He could do it as one employee to another.

Because of this, I decided to create a new position for him—ambassador. It is a one of a kind position. I had nothing to base it on; we were making it up as we went along. I believe that God has blessed us because of it.

These types of positions don't make sense from a business point of view, but they sure do make a difference in the lives of our employees, and a healthy working environment makes for better service overall.

The managers have adapted and adjusted, becoming bolder themselves. It used to be that the only encouragement I got was from Kristin and Jennifer. Now a multitude of employees encourage and invest in the vision and purpose of our company. There are so many more things we do now naturally; we don't even consciously think about it anymore.

Instead of looking with anger or frustration at unreasonable customer complaints, we decided to look at them as an opportunity to spread the gospel. You might know the expression, "Hurt people, hurt people." When someone is stressed or anxious, they often lash out at whatever target is most accessible. The service industry tends to get hit a lot.

We received a couple of customer complaints that turned into opportunities to offer prayer and counsel when we found that the real source of their upset was marital difficulties.

Another day, a customer came to our offices to complain. He was an older man, probably in his mid-sixties. His face burned with fury as he stood on the front steps and shouted his displeasure. He refused to even step foot in our office building. I met him outside, and he pulled me out to the side-walk. It's a little nerve-wracking to get pulled away like that. I had no way of knowing who he was or what he was going to do. For all I knew, he could have had a history of violence. I tried to be calm and collected as I asked him what the problem was.

After five minutes, which seemed more like an hour, he said, "Look, I just wanted to make a reservation. But your person there said they don't even take reservations! What kind of restaurant..." And he continued, his voice dripped acid.

When he caught his breath, I replied, "I'm sorry, we really don't take reservations here. I am sorry if you would have had to wait but—"

"I just wanted a special night for my aunt," he interrupted. "My mother just passed away and—" His voice caught.

There was the real point of hurt.

"—I just wanted to make it special." The edge returned to his voice. But it didn't cut the way it had at the beginning of our conversation.

"I'm so sorry about the loss of your mother. I am sure you must be really grieving right now."

I then proceeded to share the gospel and tell him about God's love during our pain.

"Do you mind if I pray for you right now?"

He nodded and we prayed together, right there on the steps of the office.

Kristin and I have a policy of praying for customers and employees who are going through hard times. We don't just say we will pray—we do it right then and there. It's a far cry from when I used to say they couldn't even write "Bless you" on a check or would sneer at people that said they were praying for me.

As Christian employees saw Kristin and I being bold and praying, it encouraged them to be bolder as well. For those who wanted to pray but felt they didn't know how, I had cards made up. I would hand them a card and say, "This is a prayer you can pray silently." And they would!

These days we always open our GM meetings on a positive note. In a recent meeting, I noticed that every single manager's positive had to do with something from a Christian perspective. They were talking about positive things they had done for the Kingdom of Christ and not for the Demos family of restaurants. It brought me to tears. What an incredible change from that first meeting that almost ended in a brawl!

I am so thankful for Ian's advice and for the opportunity I had to speak to the representative from Coca-Cola. I am thankful that God brought men like Shawn and our chaplains to work for us. He was at work in them, and He works through each of them in order to change the way we do business. He really has become our managing Director.

TEN

My Arch Nemesis

I am not the kind of guy that wants to go around collecting enemies. At least, I don't think I am. Nor do I have time to deal with "frenemies." (That is just a horrible expression.) But there was a time in my life when I successfully turned a great friend into my arch nemesis.

My father, Jim, had started a restaurant in Murfreesboro, in 1985, called Toot's. The best way to describe it is that it's a Hooters knock-off. Hooters was only two years old at the time, so the concept still seemed fairly novel.

He opened the restaurant with a couple of friends: Mike Thompson, a restaurant equipment salesman, whom he'd known for over 15 years, and Randy Freeman. Randy had worked for almost twenty years in the theatre and restaurant business with my dad. It seemed like a great partnership. This one was going to be fun. Randy was to run the restaurant, and my dad worked on the recipes for the menu.

I'm not really sure why they chose Murfreesboro and not Nashville for their flagship location; we weren't living there at the time. Maybe it had more to do with Randy and Mike than it did my dad.

Unfortunately, as can happen when friends start businesses together, Randy decided to withdraw from the partnership shortly after they opened, leaving a hole in management for my father to fill. The manager he hired quickly turned Toots into something it wasn't meant to be. In relatively short order the restaurant devolved into a sleazy bar.

"We've got to replace this guy," Mike said.

My dad completely agreed.

"My friend's son, Wade, is managing a restaurant in Memphis. You should check him out."

Dad did just that. He found Wade Hayes hard at work—a young man with a lot going for him. Dad offered Wade the job, and a little while later he agreed to come on board, moving with his wife and young children to Murfreesboro.

Wade was worth every penny he was paid. He totally turned the floundering Toots restaurant around. Toots still had a hint of the Hooters brand, but now it was family friendly. He hired both male and female servers, and while the uniform did include shorts and t-shirts, they were no longer short shorts. Basically, the whole atmosphere at Toot's changed; the food was good, the servers made the experience fun, and business increased.

I spent a lot of time at the restaurants, following my parents around, and Wade became like an older brother who took an interest in my future. When I told him I was going to Memphis State, he got excited. "My hometown! You're gonna love it." He gave me a t-shirt from when he attended there years earlier at the time Memphis went to the Final Four.

Wade was such a good worker that Mike and Dad agreed to bring him into their partnership of the restaurant and the franchising company.

When I returned from college, Wade and I grew even closer. I counted him among my best friends, practically family. He was a groomsman in my wedding, and he was at the hospital for the birth of both my children.

It was 2004 when Wade finally opened a second company-owned (non-franchise) Toots in Smyrna, Tennessee. It was a difficult opening. Most openings are; I've been through twelve so far. When you first open a restaurant, you will probably work 120 hours a week, and that's when things go well. If anything goes wrong, it will keep you up nights.

I don't exactly know what went wrong with the Smyrna opening, but it quickly fell apart.

My dad called up Bill Warman (my right-hand man at Demos') and me and said, "We really need your help...can you come?"

We knew if he was calling us, it had to be real bad; neither of us had ever worked at Toots.

We got there in the middle of the dinner rush, and it took only a couple of minutes to see that they really were in a mess. We tried to organize and offer suggestions, but things continued to worsen. Bill and I wracked our brains to fix what we saw was going wrong. We toured the kitchen and took a look at the restaurant's manuals.

Finally, we realized that not only were the manuals outdated, but also some systems just weren't working. In hindsight, I can see that the kitchen was in reverse order from the other locations, and the manuals had been designed for the way the kitchens were there. It didn't translate to the Smyrna set up.

I felt frustrated that they had gotten themselves in this predicament. My approach to the problem, however, was totally wrong. When I see a problem, I want to fight it and beat it into submission. However, the "put your head down and start swinging" tactic that I employed was taken as a personal affront to both Wade and the general manager.

Wade felt attacked. He started erecting walls between us. I was intent on knocking them down and making him see what appeared to me as common sense. I never once had the wisdom to step back and listen to him and his concerns. We just kept digging at each other, and our relationship grew further apart.

As months progressed, I took my job as "fixer" quite seriously. I went through manuals and systems, and I eventually discovered something that raised the hairs on the back of my neck. The system that was set in place for their in-store accounting was flawed. If they got audited, and they could not account for money due to this flawed system, I worried something could happen to my dad. He was getting older, there was no way I wanted him to face legal trouble because of faulty accounting. I had to protect him.

I sat down at an office computer in the common area and wrote a document that I hoped would do the trick. The only problem with it, should an issue arise, is that it would protect my father, who was not involved in the operations, but it threw Wade under the bus.

If you are going to write something like that, not that you should, a good idea is not to allow that friend see it. Unfortunately, Wade used the office computer and happened to see the letter.

"What is this?" he demanded.

I swore under my breath.

"You trying to accuse me of stealing?"

I wasn't, but looking back I can see how he would have thought that. But at that moment, I cared more about protecting my dad's interests than making peace. I had decided this mess was Wade's fault. In hindsight, I know he was doing a good job, but at the time with my youthful arrogance, I overlooked all the good that he was doing and focused only on what I perceived as his wrongdoings.

As time went on our relationship broke down so much that we couldn't work with each other. Wade tried to buy my father and Mike out, but something happened to make the purchase fall through. The problem I created bled into the relationship Wade had with my father as well.

"Why don't I take over the Smyrna franchise," I said to my parents one day. "Wade can handle the Murfreesboro one; he did well there. He can own his own business, and maybe this can bring peace."

They eventually agreed, and I got to work sorting out the mess in Smyrna. I was rather pleased with the way things were going. My right-hand man, Bill, and I were overall the franchisees, including a new one that Wade had recently brought in.

The new franchisee was a little more cunning than we had expected. He noticed that Wade and I were at odds with each other and decided to take advantage of it. He started spreading lies.

It got so bad that I was on the phone every day with our attorneys, getting advice. I had so many problems with this particular franchisee that I had no time to operate any of our businesses, and it appeared that he was teaming up with Wade to make it get worse. The stress of the situation was intense. It felt like an enormous weight had been placed on my shoulders as I tried to deal with the fallout.

Finally, we gave Wade and the new guy two choices, buy

us out or get out. We went into negotiations. Day and night, my father and I poured over paperwork on a deal, until in 2006, it was finally agreed that Wade would buy us out. It was not the deal I had hoped for, but I just couldn't take it anymore.

Tensions were so high the day of closing, Wade and his business partner would not sit in the same room with us to work out the final details. After hours of final negotiations, the paperwork was finally signed. I went out with my family for a celebratory drink and dinner. I sat with a glass in my hand, laughing almost hysterically and emotionally wrecked. I was drunk after just one drink.

It was not just the end of our partnership, it was like a particularly nasty divorce. I was closing a chapter of my life, saying goodbye to a man who had been my brother for years.

Months later, emotions continued to roil inside me. To say I was bitter is an understatement. When financial issues and sexual harassment made the Equal Opportunities Commission go after his partner, I grinned. When his partner ended up getting out of the partnership shortly after, I rejoiced in his downfall.

Even small things caused me to respond emotionally. If I drove by and saw the parking lot empty, I rejoiced. If anything good happened to him, I got angry. And I held on to this for years!

But just as Memphis brought Wade and me closer when I was younger, what happened in Memphis was about to repair a broken relationship as well. Not quite ten days after my sins were washed away in that Memphis bathroom, Kristin, Bill Warman, myself and a couple other managers, went to Chicago for one of the National Restaurant Association Restaurant shows.

They have everything from food, technology, and equipment, to indoor and outdoor furniture; anything that might be a part of a restaurant, they'll have it. You can easily walk five or six miles a day just looking at what they have in the showroom. The seminars are top notch, and there are always deals on new equipment. We try and go every two years, and I never want to miss a second of it. It is a great show.

The only minor issue I have with the show is that it opens at 9:00 am, and security is so tight they won't even let you in at 8:59. So crowds and crowds of people fill the lobby, waiting to go up to the showroom. It's been that way for as long as I can remember, and I have been attending since I was sixteen.

This particular morning, Kristin and I were waiting in the lobby for the doors to open. Bill had gone out for a smoke. The other managers were off somewhere too.

I glanced over at the bathroom that was right beside us. I really had to go, and that should kill a few minutes waiting for 9 am to roll around. I walked around the corner and saw a beautifully empty, tiled room, with a nice line of unemployed urinals. Every single one was empty. I had my pick. It was a little odd considering the thousands of people milling about the lobby, but I was totally fine with it.

I did my business and washed up. I wound my way around the walls that were framed in such as way as to replace the need for doors so fast, eager not to miss the 9 am opening, and as I turned the corner, I ran smack dab into a guy that was coming in. I hit him so hard that I had to grab onto him, like a hug, to keep from falling.

The man was Wade Hayes. The look of shock on his face was an identical reflection of my own, and we stammered through a generic greeting. It was awkward. I walked on to find my wife in the crowd, and Wade carried on into the bathroom.

"Kristin, you will never guess what just happened," I said once I reached my wife. I told her what happened and then added, "And I heard God tell me to forgive him."

The problem was that although I was a new person in Christ, the old Peter still had some sway. The old Peter did not want to deal with that awkward situation. It would be so much easier just to stop thinking horrible things about him and his business, but to have to make amends? That was different.

The very next day, just before 7:00 in the morning, before we had even gotten to the conference center, Demos' had the biggest armed robbery we had ever had at any of our restaurants.

There were four men involved in the stick-up. Two had come inside and left two getaway drivers outside. One of the robbers was an employee who had just quit and coincidentally was about to go work for Wade at Toot's. The men waited until our food delivery truck pulled up. When the back door was opened, they rushed in with guns.

Their well-planned heist was no match for God's protection services. That morning the delivery man had brought a trainee with him. A guy that supervised our prep areas also happened to be there because he didn't have his schedule and decided to go in just in case. Additionally, three more manager trainees had come in that morning.

It was more people than the thieves had bargained for. They couldn't keep track of them all. They were shouting directions, trying to round them up when the prep area supervisor took one of the trainees with him into the office and pushed the panic button.

Forty-six seconds from the time the men burst through the door, the police were there chasing after them. The two getaway drivers sped away, and the two men inside ran out into the parking as the police arrived. In a panic, the thieves started throwing money into the air, running as fast as they could towards the back street. The police gave chase, catching them before they reached the road.

Although we saw the best possible outcome (the police even caught the getaway drivers two weeks later), it was still traumatizing for the employees involved.

"Let me pray for you," I suggested once I had heard the story.

That request may have been just as traumatizing for them as the robbery itself. I had only been a Christian for a few days. Most of them hadn't even heard about new Peter yet.

When we got back to Murfreesboro, we prayed with them again and worked through some things that needed our immediate attention. There had been two armed robberies in recent years where employees were killed. I found out that the robbers had shoved a gun in the face of one of our employees, Anthony Bush, and told him to open the office door where the safes were. It was a real threat. He and the others were visibly shaken.

On top of dealing with the employees, there were police reports to deal with. It was a long few days. When we finally had some space to breathe, I realized I still hadn't done what God had asked me to do in Chicago. I needed to talk to Wade. I called him and asked if we could meet. He agreed as long as it was at his office in his restaurant. I am guessing he wanted a safe zone.

It hadn't been an easy decision for Wade to say yes to a meeting with me. He passed it by his wife first, trying to wonder what attack I had planned. But as apprehensive as he was to meet me, I was shaking in my boots to have to meet him and explain the change in me.

I am used to speaking. I have absolutely no problem holding a conversation, but that meeting was one of the hardest of my life. I was in tears. I could barely string four words together. Wade took the opportunity to share what was happening with him and how my family and I had hurt him. He was incredibly gracious to me. He forgave me and we cried together.

Although we still aren't as close as we were thirty years ago, God has brought about a restoration and healing I would never have thought possible a decade ago. He is no longer my arch nemesis, and I consider him a friend. I have no problem calling him for advice. I pull for him now. I encourage people to go to his restaurant. I am happy for him when I see the parking lot at his restaurant is full. The change in my heart is nothing short of a miracle. And I hear of him talking positively about me in the community as well. Wade could have rejected my apology, but he didn't. He showed me grace

I genuinely regret that I damaged our relationship the way I did, but I am so thankful that by being obedient to what God wanted me to do, it removed all the anger that I had. The devil can't use that as a tool against me anymore. I have heard plenty of sermons on forgiveness, and I want to testify that it's all true!

In the business world, we are taught to hate our competitors and do what we can to beat them. "Take it to the mattresses" is a business expression, first made famous in the Godfather movie. It's a way of saying, go ahead and be ruthless with your competitor—it's not personal; it's business.

I had really believed in that. I was a fighter. There was a thrill involved in it. But fighting for my way didn't help. It didn't make our restaurant or our people better. It didn't make him worse. And there is no room in our Christian walk for that sort of behavior. Jesus taught us to love our enemies.

A year or so after the robbery, we held a Bible study that Anthony Bush attended. He told us about a sentencing he had received that would require him to spend three days in jail. It was time he needed to serve at some point, and he chose that time to do it.

As he entered the cell, he recognized the man inside. It was one of the robbers—the very same guy that had put the gun in his face a year before. At that moment, Anthony knew he had to forgive him. The guy approached him hesitantly, "Do you remember me?"

Anthony nodded and said that he did. They had a chance to talk about what happened, and Anthony forgave the man that had traumatized him all those months before.

The next morning, he was told his sentence would be cut short and was released early that day. It was as if God had brought him there, just then, so that the healing work of forgiveness could happen.

Reporters sometimes ask me, "Who is your biggest competitor?" I used to say "ourselves," meaning I felt we could do better than any other restaurant as long as we performed. Now, although my answer hasn't changed, my meaning has. If our work is to glorify God, it has nothing to do with anyone else. God will take care of our success. Learning that lesson was probably the biggest thing I could have done to maintain and kickstart my relationship with Christ.

ELEVEN

The Perfect Plan

Everybody's got plans...until they get hit. —*Mike Tyson*

Peter D's, my restaurant namesake, was going to be perfect. I would do all I could to employ the right people in the right position. I would search out the right décor and spend the money to get it. I had already begun planning with men who were experts in the industry. Together we would set up a restaurant that could not fail.

From my own business studies and from working out the messes of other restaurants I had been around, I knew I could design Peter D's in a way that was easy to operate and a joy to manage. I hired a guy, who had been regional vice president at another restaurant chain, to help us run it. And I partnered with Bill Worman, who had decades of experience in the restaurant industry. Between the three of us, we had over a hundred years of operational experience in the business.

My wife, who is brilliant in her own right, understood what was trending and knew how to communicate it. We discussed the building and agreed that we weren't content to settle for just anyone locally available. We did a nationwide search for an architectural firm, willing to hire only the best. It turned out there was an exceptional firm in nearby Knoxville, Tennessee. They were perfect.

Our architect recommended a brilliant interior decorator. Kristin was in charge of the design and overall aesthetic of Peter D's, but she worked closely together with the architect and the decorator to come up with an interior that would be as beautiful as the operations made it functional.

"It looks like we have a solid plan." The decorator grinned. "Why don't you give me a call when construction is a couple of weeks out, and I'll come and put everything in place."

Perfect. It was almost too easy.

We knew just what we wanted before construction even started. We had the operations team, the architect, the designer, now all we needed was a great menu.

I worked on a menu that was sure to be a crowd pleaser, but I wasn't content to stop there. I wanted people not just to enjoy their meal, I wanted them to crave our food and think about it when they went home that night, wishing they still had a little left for a late-night snack. I wanted them to involuntarily close their eyes and savor each morsel.

So, we hired three different chefs to complement the menu that I had put together. With each chef, we went through a process to select the menu items, testing them with customers and amongst family. We rejected about 70% of the dishes put in front of us. If they weren't drool worthy, I didn't want them on the menu.

The 30% that was left still amounted to a lot of dishes. It was a perfect variety of items, from spicy and sweet to savory and comforting. We were aiming for food that was fancy with an "at home" twist. I was confident we had nailed it.

I drew up a floorplan for the restaurant that I knew would

flow perfectly. So that a server could take food from the kitchen, walk by a separate bar that would only serve the tables, pick up drink orders, and deliver it all to the tables. From there they could pick up dirty dishes and the server could drop them off at the washing station. The register would be on the same route, and they could place new orders before going back to the kitchen. It was designed for perfect efficiency. A high level of thought had gone into it so that no one would have to travel backward, interrupting the flow of service.

The kitchen plan had a similar setup. The food was assembled in front of each kitchen worker and then pushed to a central pickup point so that it would go out at precisely the right time.

Our perfect building with perfect staff would need the best and the newest equipment. We met with our point of sale company and bought state of the art, brand new everything, including a fancy system that would time the food to ensure all the dishes for a table came out at the same time. No one would have reason to complain that their meal came twenty minutes after their dates. Or that their steak was cold or their sandwich soggy. The technology would help eliminate human error.

I had become a Christian right about the time we were looking for an architect. Within days of my conversion, we had found the company in Knoxville. Not only did I have a perfect plan, but because I was now a follower of Christ, it seemed like nothing could go wrong. Life was perfect. Even when little problems cropped up, it was like the Holy Spirit was right there, assuring me that all was well. He had my back.

I gave the floorplan I had drawn up to the equipment company who put it into a CAD drawing, which is a computerized layout of the plan so that the architect could finish it up. It had every piece of equipment listed and indicated where every table was supposed to be.

When that was completed, we sent it to the architect, who planned the interior elevations; windows, beams, walls, electrics, plumbing—the works. Every minute detail was accounted for. I could see they had a good eye. I almost got butterflies thinking about how well everything was coming together.

There was a large shopping district recently built on the main road coming into Murfreesboro. Everything in that area of the city would be shiny and new. It was the perfect spot for Peter D's, and we managed to get a great plot of land right on the corner. There would be easy access and plenty of space for parking.

Since we had the best operators, the best location, the best technology, best food, best designer, and best architect, all we needed now was a great wine list. Again, I met with several professionals in the liquor and wine industry to help us draft a bar menu that was up to date and trendy. We'd have a selection of the best wines and beers available and be able to offer suggestions for pairing them with our dinner menu.

Since the new restaurant was located in our home town, we knew we would be supported by our friends and the businesses we had been working with for years. Our existing restaurant already boasted over a half million customers a year. We could only assume the town would be very friendly towards our new business.

Friends and business acquaintances often told me how

awesome it was going to be and that Murfreesboro needed a place like Peter D's. Friends and family who had been there for our menu trials often gushed over how good the food was. And I agreed that it was good. Murfreesboro did need us.

Besides, God was on our side. How could we fail? I had begun praying a lot for the success of Peter D's. Part of my perfect plan, which was made before I became a believer, was that we would close on Mondays, allowing managers to have a better quality of life. Mondays were the slowest day in the restaurant business.

But one day as I was praying it was like God asked me, "Why are you closing on a Monday? Why won't you close on Sundays and offer that day to me."

It sounded a lot like restaurant suicide, but I really felt that God was directing me and I trusted that He would back us up. Little did I realize God is not back up. He is in control—not anyone or anything else.

With Peter D's I had done everything by the book. We were a shoe-in for success. I had studied gazillions of business books; I could even quote them to you. I read so many through the years that I could probably write a book on writing the perfect business book.

If their authors knew the time and attention to detail that I put in, handpicking the right team and sparing no expense on the restaurant's inner workings, they would see that there was nothing that I did that would point toward failure. I was back in control as the managing director.

But there was one element that had snuck into my plans, that no business book addresses that would prove to be my downfall—pride.

TWELVE

The Snowball

It was supposed to be routine, one of the many regular construction inspections just to make sure we were on track. I walked with the inspector around the poured concrete floors and the curbs that showed where the walls were going to be. Something was off. The more I looked and walked off the space, the more I could see that something was very wrong. We were short on space. Not just a little short, there were numerous feet missing in the foundation.

Could I have drawn the plans wrong? I was so sure about them before. I had been meticulous. Maybe the contractor had gotten it wrong. I waved him over.

"We're coming up short here. Can I see the plans you're using?"

I had caught him off guard. But he was confident in his work. "We've been working to spec. If there's a problem, it isn't on our end."

He went to grab the plans, and I stood in the center of the concrete pad, baffled. I hoped he was wrong. He wasn't. When we compared the plans, we saw that they matched the specifications. I couldn't believe we had gotten it so wrong.

"It's not going to work. We'll need to reconfigure the space." Each word that came out of my mouth stung my pride.

We took out some tracing paper and tried to redraw the space. The only way we could see how to make it work was to take out a wall. Even then we would lose at least twelve seats in the restaurant. Loss of seats means an instant loss of revenue. But it was too late to start over, we would have to just push on with the revised plan.

I received a call one day. "Peter? We have a problem."

It was a greeting I was getting used to. "What is it?"

"The beams have come in, but there are way more than we can possibly fit."

I groaned. Those beams were expensive. I assured the contractor I would be there right away and braced myself for what I would have to deal with. The walls were up, and I had started to feel hopeful, but obviously I shouldn't have.

I toured the construction site, grimacing as the contractor pointed out the flaws in the design. Not only did we have more beams than we could use, but also some of them would go right into the windows. The placement of them made no sense. But again, at this point in the build, there wasn't much we could do.

Again, I got a call with the usual greeting. "It's the equipment. None of it is fitting."

It's normal to encounter problems as you build, but this was beyond the normal amount that you account for. My head ached; the muscles in my shoulders had turned into stone. The kitchen equipment was way too large for the space. We could squeeze in the essentials, but the things I had ordered that were going to make work life so much easier for my staff would have to go. We would even have to make do with fewer garbage cans; there just wasn't space.

The range hoods went up next. Again, they were way too

big. The vents weren't even over the stove, they were too far out. They were meant to be positioned in a way that would suck up steam and smoke from the cooktops. The fans were powerful enough, but they would be sucking air from the floor. I couldn't stop kicking myself. How could I have made these many mistakes?

Finally, the bar and its equipment came in. It too didn't fit. In a way, I was almost glad they didn't. This proved it wasn't my fault. I had used the exact same plan for a bar that I had worked at in Nashville. I remember making sure to draw it to the exact same specifications. I couldn't be the only one to blame. I needed to see our award-winning architect. Maybe they could pinpoint where things had gone wrong.

"The building just doesn't match the plans we had made."

I laid out what I had in front of him, and he pulled out the plans his firm had worked on.

"Look." I tapped the paper between us, "We have a trash compactor that won't even fit into the room built for it."

We both frowned at the paper, trying to see where it all went wrong. He tugged a sheet of paper from underneath and placed it on top. The equipment plan had matched perfectly with the plan I had drawn up. He placed the blueprints they had drawn up on top.

At first glance, it looked exactly the same. And then we found the reason behind all the problems—the scale was off on their blueprints. Instead of a quarter inch scale, they assumed it was a three-eighths of an inch scale. That meant that for every foot of the building they had drawn, it was off by an inch, multiply that by thousands of square feet, and you end up with thousands of square inches lost.

I was beyond frustrated. This error early on had cost us thousands of dollars, and the loss of floor space in the restaurant would continue to lose us thousands in potential revenue. We were only weeks away from opening. We couldn't tear it all down and start again.

"I can't understand how this wasn't caught earlier in inspections."

The architect shook his head and replied, "We have pictures from the earlier inspections, but it seems like some of them failed to take measurements at the time."

So, what he was telling me was that not only did they not catch their mistake on the front end, their lack of controls during the building process meant it snowballed into what it was today. I was furious. I had to do some heavy duty praying just to lower my blood pressure and come out of that meeting without bloodshed.

I took a deep breath. At least we could still make the place look good. It may not be as highly functional as I had planned, but we could figure it out.

When the drywall was up, Kristin and I toured the pace. We could see that despite everything, Peter D's still had the potential to be a really great restaurant. "It's a little early still, but you should probably call the decorator and let him know we are ready for him. We don't want to take any more chances on things going wrong or taking longer than they should."

Kristin took out her cell phone and punched in his number, "Hi! This is Kristin Demos, from Peter D's. We just wanted to let you know that we're ready. We're so excited for y'all to get started, so we can see it all in place."

There was a brief silence on the other end and then came

five words that made our stomachs clench. "You mean you were serious?"

"I'm sorry?"

He had to be kidding. "I took another job, I didn't know you were serious."

He didn't know we were serious?! Do a lot of people make plans and hire him as a joke? Wasn't he a critically acclaimed decorator, recommended by our architectural firm?

Kristin spluttered through the rest of the short conversation, but nothing changed the fact that our decorator had flaked out on us.

Kristin looked at me aghast. "What are we going to do?"

"Can you do it?"

"What about the hiring, we have a load of interviews lined up."

I almost chuckled. How much more could go wrong? "I'll take care of the hiring if you take care of the decorating."

Kristin had a little experience in decorating. Even if she wasn't a professional, I had more faith in her than I did in any pros. I took out my business card and a credit card and handed them to her. "Let's just get it done."

Kristin got right to work. She couldn't get the special rates that professional designers could so she decided to branch out and track down pieces from all over the place. Antique stores and eBay supplemented what she could find in interior decoration stores. She worked liked crazy for the next fourteen days.

By the time we were set to open, she had managed to get about 80% of the restaurant decorated. It looked good. Really good. It would be impossible to duplicate the décor because the majority of the show-stopping pieces she had picked up were rare finds. We blew the budget, and then some; but if it wasn't for Kristin, I have no earthly idea what I would have done.

Unfortunately, because Kristin was tied up with the decorating, she wasn't able to sit in on the interviews for new employees.

At Demos' we like hiring new staff without experience because we can train them up without having to deal with any prior bad habits. It works at Demos' because they are joining a team with experience. Unfortunately, we carried the practice over to Peter D's, which meant 70% of our serving staff had no experience at all.

To make matters worse, at the same time as we were trying to hire for Peter D's, we lost half of our general managers at Demos'. That had never happened before. We would lose staff here and there for various reasons, but we had never before lost so many in so short a space of time. This meant that I would be even more stretched trying to work things out at our other locations.

I was glad I had given my life over to Jesus because it felt like everything around me was crumbling, and I needed to cling to Him just to get through the day. My faith was still quite new, I was struggling to make decisions on my own but didn't realize all that I could trust God for.

Our opening was just over a week away, but it seemed wise to do a soft opening earlier and try and work out some of the kinks we were bound to have. With so many of our staff new to the restaurant industry and with a brand-new system in place, it would give everyone a chance to get some practice in. We would open for a few hours over lunch and again for a few hours at supper time.

A week before our big opening weekend, we opened our doors to the public. It was a disaster.

Because the equipment was too big for the kitchen and we had lost so much space, the recipes and instructions we would typically put on the wall wouldn't fit. They would have to be pulled out and referred to until they were memorized. We didn't even have space for plates.

Usually we would have space by the grills for the plates, but instead, the cooks would need to put the food on a pass plate, which would then get handed to someone who assembled the food to go out. Not ideal.

The first orders came in, and we discovered that the majority of our servers didn't know how to use the register. Several of them were gathered around it scratching their heads.

Crash! Another server dropped a tray of drinks. He scrambled to clean it up. Customers were getting impatient.

Our Director of Operations, with all his years of experience, didn't seem to have the ability to organize and communicate clearly. He was like the dog from the cartoon Up, chasing squirrels. He ran from one disaster to the next, never resolving any of them.

"It's burnt. It can't go out. Do it again." Our kitchen manager was ticked. Time after time, orders were either burnt or undercooked.

It was a terrible opening. We all knew it. I was glad we had only committed to a short lunchtime and dinner service. We later reviewed some of the things that had gone on, excusing much of it as opening day problems and resolving to do better the next day. We didn't. If possible, it was worse.

I reviewed some of the CCTV footage to try and pinpoint

where our most significant problems were. I saw one of the servers drop a tray for no apparent reason. One minute they were standing there with the tray balanced on their hand, the next moment they turned their hand and the tray came crashing down. Most of the servers didn't even seem to know how to hold a tray. It was also apparent that the majority of the servers didn't know how to input the orders in the first place.

"How did these guys even pass the server tests?" I asked the area supervisor. It didn't matter how great our system was if the staff didn't know how to work within it.

He shook his head, "I haven't had a chance to grade them yet."

My eyes nearly bugged out of my head. "So, we don't know if they're ready to be on the floor. Obviously, they aren't."

I took a look at the tests. The majority of our servers had failed, and their training was woefully incomplete.

This guy had brilliant ideas, in many ways we were blessed to have him on staff, but for an area supervisor, he had no idea how to supervise all that he needed to.

By our fifth shift, I could see that our general manager was really struggling. She had cried every shift so far. She is amazing and could have taken over any one of our existing stores and done brilliantly, but Peter D's with all its issues was proving too much. It was giving her a nervous break-down.

"We need to do something about the grills and fryers. We can't seem to get the temps right."

Our kitchen manager was stressed. The constantly burnt food reflected poorly on him. It was also unusual. We'd never had this problem at our other restaurants. Besides, the new system was supposed to ensure this didn't happen.

"We'll bring over some guys from Demos' to help you out," I told them. Experienced cooks should be able to sort out most of the issues. It didn't help. They too had trouble with the equipment. When I walked by, I could see the cooktops were really dark, an indicator that the temp was too high. But the temp gauge said otherwise. They were all set to the correct settings, and a check of the thermostats showed that they were all fine.

It took some more in-depth investigation before the real problem was found. It had nothing to do with the actual equipment. The problem was the gas regulator—you know, the big round metal thing you see outside of buildings. Because the regulator was broken, there was no way to control how much gas was coming in.

Sometimes the gas would come in at such force that it would boost the temps on our grills and fryers to six or seven hundred degrees, and then suddenly the temperature would drop to two hundred. Because of this, we couldn't judge how long food would take to cook.

As you can imagine, a gas regulator isn't something you can buy at a hardware or equipment store. It needed to be specially ordered. In hindsight, we should have closed and regrouped, but I didn't. I still tried to train people on the malfunctioning grill.

"Come on, guys, let's pull together. We can do this, right?"

It wasn't exactly a motivational talk, but it was the best I could summon all things considered. There was reluctant agreement as we pushed forward towards our grand opening.

There were other issues of course; our sound equipment had been installed according to the equipment plans instead of the architectural ones. This meant that in some areas the music was too loud to hold a conversation, and in others, it was so quiet you couldn't really hear it. Another expensive fix. We were completely out of funds. Our budget was decimated by our problems, but it didn't stop them from coming.

People couldn't find our restaurant, even when they knew where it was supposed to be. The only place we were to place our street sign, according to local authorities, was in a spot entirely hidden by a street sign, telephone pole, and electrical box. You couldn't even see it until you had passed the turn.

Our kitchen manager had some emotional issues that were taking a toll on his performance. He was having troubles at home, he said. We only found out later that his marital problems were due to an affair he was having with one of our servers.

In a way, I think it was important that things with Peter D's fell apart. I hated every stressful minute of the experience, but if everything had gone according to my "perfect plan," I would definitely have taken the credit. My pride would have kept hold of me, and I wouldn't have learned to rely on and trust in God the way that I did.

THIRTEEN

A Very Black Friday

If you, or perhaps your child, have ever been in a play, you might be familiar with the old wives' tale that terrible dress rehearsals make for great opening nights. If that translated over to restaurants, then our opening weekend should have gone perfectly.

Our soft-opening had been fraught with problems; there was the burnt food, untrained servers who didn't even know how to take an order, malfunctioning equipment, and stressed out management. Customer complaints poured in; sometimes because the servers failed to ring in their food, sometimes because they rang it in incorrectly, and often because their orders came out either undercooked or burnt.

We had tried to muddle through by apologizing, doing our best to appease, muscling through the problems, and jerry-rigging things to work in ways they hadn't been built for, all before our official opening weekend.

By Thursday night, we had seen business slowly pick up, and I really did not want it to get any busier; we were not ready for them. I hoped and prayed that despite all the setbacks, things would actually work out for us on our first night of the weekend.

When I opened my eyes on the morning of our grand-opening, my throat was on fire, my muscles ached, my head was burning, and my hands were like ice. I tried to take a couple of ibuprofen, but I could barely swallow. Not a good sign. I knew all week that something was trying to come on me; I could feel it build. My body was just too exhausted to fight it.

I climbed into the shower, hoping the steam would clear my sinuses. Today was not a day that I could forsake the restaurant and stay curled up in bed. The shower helped, but only for a few minutes; before I was even out the door, my congestion was back, full-force.

Before I even reached Peter D's, I was getting frantic calls. I would have to hit the ground running.

"Father," I prayed, "You gotta help me. I can barely stay on my feet."

A few people gave me concerned looks as I walked in, but no one suggested I go home and sleep it off. No matter how empathetic, we all knew that it was all hands on deck.

The lunch service did not go well, but it could have been worse. At least, that's what we were about to learn. When dinner service started, customers literally flooded in. That hadn't happened before, and it caught us off guard.

The workers at the host stand panicked, unable to keep up with all the names being yelled at them. In their confusion, they wrote down the wrong pager numbers, or the same pager number for multiple customers, or handed the pager to the wrong person. The resulting chaos was enough to make frustrated customers outraged before we even got them seated.

When our servers finally managed to input their orders, the kitchen couldn't keep up with the backlog. No one in the kitchen was taking control. The kitchen staff was irritated with pretty much everyone and everything. You could feel the negative energy pouring off them, making the small kitchen feel even smaller than it was.

Plates were stacked haphazardly, one on top of the other, on any available surface. There just wasn't enough room for the cooks to assemble the food. Panic started to twist at my stomach, but I remembered the words of my mother, "If you start to panic, move off to the side so no one can see you."

I looked around for a quiet corner, but there was nowhere to go! I took a breath, attempting to calm the fingers of fear that grasped my throat and weakened my knees. I exhaled slowly, looking around, assessing how I could help.

The massive exhaust hood, which was too big for the original kitchen plan, was so large it sucked away the sound of voices. Everyone was shouting, but no one was hearing each other. Before long, the kitchen completely went down. It wasn't really their fault for theirs was an impossible mission. Panic and fear started to be replaced by helplessness.

Our servers were also uniquely inept that night, taking ten to fifteen minutes just to ring in the food. This, combined with the forty or so minutes that the kitchen was taking to get orders out, meant that each order was taking an average of fifty-two minutes from the time the order was placed to the time the food arrived at the table. That was just the average time! Half of the customers had to wait even longer. And in most cases, after customers had waited almost an hour, if their food wasn't burnt or ice cold, the orders were wrong.

I walked back to the cook's line and took a few moments to assess where it was all going wrong. If I couldn't figure out where to help, maybe I could stop a problem that was the cause of many other problems. The difficulty in pinpointing a place to start was that things were going wrong at every point in the process. Half of me wanted to cry, and the other half wanted to start cussing and throwing things like I used to do.

I rubbed my forehead, trying to clear my fuzzy, aching brain. I was running strictly on the adrenaline my body had reserved for opening day. I prayed it was enough to help me take control and straighten things out.

The harder and faster each person tried to work, the larger the mess they created for the team as a whole. I watched our two strongest supervisors working in the midst of the people, trying to fix things when neither had worked this system or this menu before. They just couldn't stay on top of all the issues. We needed a General leading this battle. Someone had to take control. That someone was going to have to be me.

"I want everyone to stop working right now!" I screamed at the top of my aching lungs.

About half of the kitchen staff heard and paused what they were doing, looking at me like they weren't sure what I'd said. I tried again, this time shouting individual names and screaming for them to stop.

"STOP WORKING! EVERYONE STOP!"

It was like a game of freeze. The sound of plates on metal counters and the scraping and clanging of spatulas on grills abruptly ceased.

We were going to do what I do in life when I am overwhelmed. "We are going to take it one ticket at a time," I screamed. "Start with one ticket and do it right. One at a time."

They continued to look at me like I was crazy, but they followed my instructions. I was sending food out the kitchen, one table at a time. If someone tried to work a second ticket, I would shout their name.

"Trell! Stop, right there! We aren't moving on until this ticket is done, and we've done it right!"

One table at a time, we worked through the orders. If there was an item missing that we needed, we would stop, throw all that food out, and start over from the beginning so food wouldn't go out cold.

Working that slowly and methodically was painful. One table at a time, over and over. I have never before or since had a shift in the restaurant go that badly.

"Hey, Mr. Demos?" A cook approached me later, "That was the coolest thing I have ever seen an owner do."

It was just a few words, but I felt relief flood my stressed body. I had worried I had ticked them all off, that they would have been offended at my micromanaging that night. It was a relief to know that he at least knew I had done what needed to be done.

While I was in the kitchen, Kristin, poor thing, was out on the floor handling all the customer complaints in person. It was her first time in that role. She got thrown into it on the worst of nights. She had to appease tables that were annoyed before they sat down and furious over the lack of competent service and the long waits. She had her work cut out for her, trying to repair the reputation we had built up at Demos' over the past twenty-plus years.

When I crawled into bed that night, even though my mind attempted to replay each and every failure, illness and fatigue dragged me into unconscious oblivion. I wish I could have stayed in that space for a few weeks. When I woke up the next morning, I felt beat up. Kristin hadn't slept well either. She was anxious.

"What are we going to do?" she asked more than once.

I had no idea how to answer her. Since our problems began, I had concentrated a lot of mental energy on coming up with a plan to fix things. When she asked again that morning, I realized I still didn't have any answers. I had come up with a couple of band-aid solutions, but nothing that would really fix things if we got busy again.

I went to work with the weight of last nights failure heavy on me. We just needed to get through this Saturday, and we could take a little time to try and regroup while we were closed on Sunday. We would take it slow and seat fewer tables, giving the kitchen a chance to keep up. That was the only band-aid I could offer.

I thought about all the angry customers Kristin had faced the night before and recalled the look in her eyes as she watched me work in the kitchen. I figured I should call her up and encourage her with my plan. If I could comfort her, it may help me have a little hope as well.

"Hello?" Kristin's voice still had that note of concern.

"I figured it out. I know what we can do!" I was not being 100% truthful, but I really wanted to comfort and take care of her. In reality, I was scared of losing everything; a night like we just had would never be fixed by one or two band-aids. It required invasive surgery.

As I started to explain "my solution," my brain recognized the deception. Suddenly a lump rose in my throat. I walked out the backdoor of the restaurant and into the open field behind. I didn't get very far when I broke down in tears.

"Oh, Peter—" Kristin's voice was warm and comforting but hard to hear over my sobs.

"We're going to get through this. Things will work out."

I nodded, even though she couldn't see me and wept as

she continued to comfort me, unable to get words past the lump in my throat.

When I finally hung up, I walked into the woods beyond the clearing and sat down on a stump, crying and praying.

"Father, it's all gone wrong. I don't know what to do. Help us, please."

I told God all about my disappointments and frustrations, wondering why He hadn't stepped in to fix it all. What had I done wrong?

We scraped by on Saturday and made some changes while we were closed on Sunday so that the following week would be better, but it was far from being what it should be.

Over the next month, the financial statements came out. I had planned for a loss, it's a wise thing to do when opening a restaurant, but the amount I had accounted for the year, we had lost in one month. I was shocked and decided I must have made a mistake, so I checked the numbers again. It didn't require more than a quick glance to tell me that we really lost this money. The next month I lost even more than the first. In two months we had doubled the loss that I had anticipated for the entire first year.

I was numb. I couldn't see how we would have enough cash to stay open, but there was nothing we could do about that until we started fixing the operations.

"I think we need to pay ahead on our mortgage and utilities. That way, if we go under, we will have a couple of months before we need to worry."

I hated that we had to think about this possibility. Having this conversation with Kristin was one of the hardest conversations I could have had. I felt like I was telling my wife that she married a failure. Nothing I had done lately had gone right.

The online complaints started next. You know the type, people who choose a snappy pseudonym like @partygirl097 or @yormama_13 (Not their real names. If you know a @partygirl097 or @yormama_13, please note that I am not actually talking about them.) and tear you apart on YELP with creatively spelled curse words and bad grammar. What is really frustrating about some of these complaints is that they came from the same people who would verbally tell us everything was great and they loved the food, when we stopped at their table.

I remembered talking to a young couple at one table who had not finished their food. I asked if everything was okay. "Oh, yes. It was great. We're just full." They assured me.

"Are you sure, because if there was anything that we could have done—"

"No, no, really. Everything was fine." They smiled and started to gather their things. And so, I believed them.

The next day, my heart sunk, next to a fresh, one-star review was a picture of the woman who had been "just too full to finish it all."

At first, we took every complaint at face value. We believed people if they told us there was a problem with service, and they hadn't seen a server in over half an hour. We began researching the complaints, trying to see how best to fix them. The first step, of course, is determining at which point in their visit the problem took place. But as we researched, we discovered that some of the complaints weren't actually true. In fact, many of them weren't even close to being true.

One complaint that had come from a good friend of my sister was particularly worrying. She said it took forever for their table to be waited on; and when they finally were, the food came out cold. She even went so far as to call me out by name, saying she hadn't seen me in the restaurant at all. My sister, when she heard, was upset and embarrassed that her friend had been treated so poorly.

I was shocked. I knew that we still had some problems, but I had thought we had rectified a lot of the things she had complained about.

I decided to look at the CCTV footage of her visit so we would know how to correct the server and any staff who hadn't been doing their jobs. The video footage was fascinating...some might even say, revealing.

She was right in saying that her server wasn't doing a good job. I agree but not because she was absent. The server had stopped by their table too many times. She visited the table twelve times during the course of their visit, double what our policy suggests. Their food came out quickly and not only that, a manager and I both visited their table. Every detail of her complaint was revealed to be a bald-faced lie. My sister couldn't believe it,

"She wouldn't do that. She has no reason to lie."

"Honestly, come look for yourself."

She did come. And she too was shocked. Why would a friend feel the need to bash us like that for no reason?

Another complaint came in about a manager who had, apparently, just dropped the customer's food on the table without a word and stalked off. When I first read that, my anger flared. I was ready to tear a strip off that manager. It is an action you might possibly expect from a stressed-out newbie, but our managers were well trained and generally very good with customers.

Something prompted me to check the video again so I could judge for myself if they had acted inappropriately. Again, we saw that the complaint was fabricated. The manager had brought the food, but they had placed it carefully in front of each client and spent about a minute chatting with them at the table. They even stopped by the table again later. As we investigated other complaints, we discovered some of the "reviewers" had never even visited the restaurant. Since then, I've learned that some restaurants will have their employees write negative reviews about other restaurants in order to bring down the new business. A sly move but dirty.

We went back to these customers online to challenge their complaint. Let me tell you, that made things a hundred times worse. Now we had people up in arms over the fact that we had challenged a customer's reviews and opinions. They said that Kristin, who was the one handling most of the complaints, had a lot to learn from my mother, who often had the same role at Demos'.

After getting so many false complaints, it started to make me feel that all of them are not true. Besides, no one wants to admit that they are performing badly, especially someone like me who was naturally good at his job.

One of the many recurring complaints was that we didn't serve ice in our water. We had decided early on that we would use double filtered water in a chilled bottle. We still offered ice but didn't automatically serve it that way.

Filtered water in chilled bottles was a new concept in Murfreesboro but was common in neighboring Nashville and other cities in the US. Because we were the first in the city to serve it this way, people were furious. One man even stopped Kristin and the kids at the square in town to yell at her about it.

Another common complaint came from customers telling me what a horrible human being I was for competing with my father. They didn't realize that my dad had sold Demos' to me years ago, and by that point, I had been operating it longer than my parents had. They would literally yell at me for competing with him. In fact, people still come up to me today to tell me that they ate at my father's restaurant but haven't tried mine yet.

We had never been under fire like this before. It really felt like people were out to get us. As a result, we started to handle complaints poorly. We had begun to assume that the majority of online complaints were lies. We didn't waste any time checking them out or talking to staff about them. Sometimes we wouldn't even respond. This meant that real problems weren't being addressed, so they became much worse.

When people got angry with us on social media, we felt like we could deal with it. We didn't like it, but at least we could decide not to look. But when that man yelled at Kristin and the kids in the town square, and when we continued to get angry complaints no matter where we went, be it grocery stores, parking lots, or the movie theatre, we felt a little afraid to go out in public.

For a while, we ended up going to Nashville or outlying areas when we left our house because we really were afraid that people would do something to us. The hostility was so intense, we even considered moving out of the city.

Do you remember I told you about all the friends that had applauded us for opening Peter D's? Many had come to the various tastings, offered us advice on what we should do with the business, made menu suggestions, and were really excited about it. So, when they came, and it wasn't what they envisioned, they got angry about it.

Some seemed offended we hadn't incorporated some of their specific suggestions. Some said it was because I had gotten too spiritual. Some, it seemed, could see the train wreck Peter D's was becoming and didn't want to have anything to do with it. Friendships we had thought were solid, fell apart.

The restaurant was struggling, and our relationships were now floundering. What else? Our finances were in shambles.

The bankers who had loaned us the money to open Peter D's came in and seeing how slow we were, started asking me questions. Because they were asking questions, I got nervous. I knew our financials were not good; it doesn't take a genius to see all the empty tables in the middle of the dinner rush and put two and two together. I was just waiting for these men to start adding to my problems.

EVERYTHING I had put my security in was getting slowly stripped away. Apart from my family, God had spared me that worry, at least.

My original plan had been to be active in Peter D's for six weeks and then pull myself out and leave it to the Area Supervisor, freeing me to supervise the Area Supervisors for Peter D's and Demos'. It was clear now that wasn't going to happen.

Fear was wanting to take hold. I had to stand firm and not go back to the old comfortable way of doing things and allow fear to take over. Learning to trust during times of stress is very hard, but it is something I must have to do. Some days I had to talk with God about it many times a day, and other days not as frequently. Regardless, I know He has it. I had to get out of His way.

FOURTEEN

Now Serving Breakfast

"You will never make it six months." I was hearing that warning a lot, and I didn't know how to reply. No matter how many band-aids we applied to our problems, we were still bleeding money. Our debt was mounting. I wanted to be hopeful and have faith that God would help bring us out of this financial free fall, but the truth was I wasn't sure we would last six months either.

We were still having trouble getting the food to come out the way it was supposed to. Our reservation system had crashed and burned on its first busy day. Customers were so angry they threw their pagers at me—they were bouncing them off the host, hitting me or my outstretched hand. I was upset to see them leave, but to be honest, I was relieved too; it took a little pressure off.

When I found out that many of our servers hadn't passed the test or waited tables before, I knew I would have to do for them what I had done in the kitchen on opening night. I was going to have to micromanage. Nobody likes that word, especially not me, but I couldn't see any other choice. We had begun to pay attention to details and customer comments, many of which revolved around service.

The business we had lost in those first weeks wasn't coming back. It was time to apply pressure to the wound. I got myself a stopwatch and stood behind the register, timing the servers as they entered orders. We had to get those times down. The added pressure did help them finally learn the register from A to Z, which allowed the customer to get their food faster. Another minor success.

Next, I called our rep from Mobil Fixtures, our equipment company. He toured the restaurant and came up with some suggestions on layout and equipment that would work in the space. It would cost us a lot of money for new equipment, but it would be much more user-friendly. At the top of the list, we needed a new set of fryers, ones that fit properly and could keep up with demand. Those things don't come cheap. But fortunately, the ones we had were almost new. We could sell them and redeem some of the cost on the replacements.

It wasn't long after we put them up for sale that a buyer came along. She didn't even argue on the price, she just happily handed over a cashier's check for thousands of dollars. It took us a few days before we cashed it and found out it was forged. A bitter disappointment.

Around this same time, it became clear that we needed to separate with our director of operations. As much as we liked his ideas and vision, running Peter D's, with all its many challenges, was just too much for him to handle. In fact, it was too much for any one person. We replaced him with a couple of people from Demos', one for the kitchen and one for the front. With their wealth of experience of our standards and systems, things began to operate the way they were meant to.

We weren't 100% consistent, but we were stabilizing and starting to see a few minor successes. Food was getting out on time, and servers now knew how to carry a tray. Basic things that are normal for restaurants were great feats to be celebrated.

However, one area we weren't making any progress on was the financials. Every month we still carried major losses. We just couldn't get enough people through the doors to compensate for our costs. The damage to our reputation was out there. People weren't willing to try us again, and some wouldn't even try us the first time because our reputation was so appalling. Frequently, I would feel the sting of people saying, "I like Demos', but I haven't tried your place because I have never heard anything good about it." I am sure they didn't mean to be as hurtful as they were. To them, it was probably just idle chatter about area restaurants. But for me, it was a stab in the gut every time.

Every day, I would start my morning, by waking up with dread and checking my emails on my phone, hoping there weren't any new online reviews. If I got a message about a review, I was petrified to open it. It took all my courage to click it open.

Throughout the day and night, if people asked Kristin or I if we owned Peter D's, we were hesitant to say yes, mentally preparing ourselves for a verbal thrashing or instant disapproval. All the stress and all the lies had taken their toll on us from the moment we woke up until we climbed into bed at night. There were many days when I just laid there with my eyes open, knowing my only reward was a cup of coffee and spending time with the Lord in my daily Bible reading.

At first, we were getting a lot of two- or three-star reviews. Slowly and methodically by listening carefully and fixing the serious problems, we got most of the new ratings up to four, sometimes even five stars! It was painfully tedious, demanding work, trying everything we could to cut costs without losing customers.

Fortunately, when the going got tough, I got tougher. Comments that said we wouldn't make it six months made me want to fight hard to hold it together. And it was working; things were starting to turn around. It still wasn't great, but it was manageable.

"I'm going to loan some more money to the business to get it back up to where it needs to be," I told Kristin. "If we can just get through to Christmas, we should be able to pull out of it."

It was October. Christmas was only a couple of months away, and by the end of the month, the shopping center right next to us would be decorating for the holidays. People will soon start their Christmas shopping.

"We should be able to tap into the Christmas market and pull out of this."

Kristin smiled hopefully, but I wasn't too sure how true her hope really was.

"You know what I've noticed lately?" she asked, "we're getting a lot of repeat customers from Franklin and Mt. Juliet."

Franklin and Mt. Juliet were nearby towns about a thirty-minute drive from us. Murfreesboro may not be supporting us, but it was nice to know we could count on the neighbors.

"Interesting, isn't it? I noticed too that we are holding a lot of children's birthday parties. That's a little odd, don't you think? It's not like we've put any special effort in to be kid friendly."

Kristin nodded. "It's true. That is a bit weird."

"But, hey. I'm not complaining."

As long as people paid, we were happy to see and accept anyone.

Kristin sighed. We were both tired and weary of fighting an uphill battle. Looking at my personal financials, I was scared. The money I had loaned the business before was all dried up. I was about to advance another hefty sum that I had no confidence I would ever see it again. The money I had put into the business was likely to disappear when we had to close the restaurant. What if we lost our home over this?

I figured out our average loss and loaned more money to get us through to February. If we could just make it that long, we would have at least made it more than six months. I just wanted to last longer than all the nay-sayers were expecting. And we were now moving in the right direction, so there was a slim amount of hope. Very slim.

Hope disappeared early one Saturday morning. I had been having trouble sleeping, but the last night was particularly bad. Problems always seem greater and more overwhelming at night, and I found that I was afraid for tomorrow, terrified in fact.

As I lay there with my eyes open, I wanted to resort to the old Peter way—to get angry and come out swinging at everyone who was in my way. But I knew that wasn't right. I kept hearing, "You have to turn it over to Jesus." What does that even mean in real life? Not wanting to wake Kristin, I climbed quietly out of bed, got dressed, and headed to the office to read my Bible, desperately needing some answers.

I sat at my worktable across from my desk with my cup of coffee and started reading. I couldn't concentrate long enough to make sense of the words. I closed my eyes and tried to pray. As I was praying, overwhelming feelings of worry and fear suddenly gripped me. I started sobbing. I cried so hard, in fact, that I fell on the floor next to that little round table I was reading at. I was inconsolable. I couldn't stop crying like a small child gasping for breaths between the sobs. My lungs burned as they inhaled deep wracking breaths; my eyes grew puffy and red. My nose dripped on the rug, but I didn't care. My life was in ruins, and God was doing nothing about it.

Suddenly, I heard a voice say, "That's enough! Get up and go to work."

The voice was so strong and loud that I was sure someone had come into the office, not a comforting thought. It was about five o'clock by this time; no one else was meant to come in right then. The voice was not recognizably anyone's that worked for us, but it was still oddly familiar. There was no sound of breathing or footsteps in the hall, nor any other human noises that the ear picks up when you are alone in a building.

I immediately stopped crying, looked around, and then I obeyed. It was like someone had just said, "Stop it, now." Not unkindly but matter-of-factly and very direct. I pushed myself up from the floor, grabbed my Bible, and sat back down at my desk.

For a few seconds, maybe even minutes, I did nothing. I was so emotionally drained, I couldn't do anything. I sat in front of my computer totally drained.

The easiest thing I could do was answer some emails. I was sure there would be hundreds demanding my attention. I could start there. I clicked on the little letter icon and opened my inbox. For almost ten minutes, my fingers flew across the keyboard responding to a myriad of queries in spite of the fog in my brain and the fact I did not want to be there at all. Then, a memory sprang to mind of something that had happened when Kristin was pregnant with our daughter, years before I was saved.

There had been many complications throughout her pregnancy, at one point Kristin even needed to be rushed to the hospital. We arrived with fear and trembling and rushed to the reception. There on the wall of the intake window, I saw this verse, "Do not worry about tomorrow, tomorrow has enough worries of its own" (Matthew 6:34 paraphrase). Even though that incident had happened ten years before, I could still remember the handwriting and the color of the paper.

It had to be God, calling that moment, that image, to mind. I grabbed my Bible and started reading in Matthew 6,

That's why I'm telling you, don't be anxious about your life, what you'll eat or what you'll drink... Isn't life more than food, and the body more than clothing? Look at the birds of the air: they don't plant. They don't harvest. And yet your heavenly Father feeds them. Aren't you more valuable than a bird? And who on earth, can add a single hour to his lifespan, by being anxious? ... So, don't be anxious, saying, 'What shall we eat?' or 'What shall we drink?' or 'What shall we wear?' ...your heavenly Father knows that you need them all. But seek first the kingdom of God and his righteousness, and all these things will be added to you" (Matthew 6:25-33 author paraphrase).

As I read, something in me shifted. I had a strong assurance that God held me, and He was never going to let me hit rock bottom. It was as if He had tied a bungee cord around my ankles, and although I could see the rocks below, I knew He was going to snatch me up again in some direction, maybe not the direction I wanted, but He wasn't going to let me hit the rocks below.

The verses in Matthew led me to Philippians 4:6,

Do not be anxious about anything, but in every situation, by prayer and petition, with thanksgiving, present your requests to God (NIV).

I wasn't being thankful.

My family wasn't the only one affected by the happenings at Peter D's. Many of the managers and employees were also worried about what the future held for them. We all needed to switch our focus back to the One who could save us. I wrote up an email inviting all managers and employees for a time of prayer and thanksgiving that Sunday. I made up posters and talked to Peter D's staff and our chaplain. I had no idea what to expect, or who might come. It might just be just the chaplain and me. But we would pray and give thanks to God for His goodness. That Sunday about fifteen people showed up. Together we spent time thanking God and worshipping Him for everything that came to mind. We then invited God to give us ideas.

"Father God, our ideas and our fixes aren't working. Please show us another way. Give us ideas that can be used to turn things around."

I left hopeful, excited even, to see what God had in store for us for the next week.

The following week came, and our sales numbers were the worst we had ever seen. It was discouraging for some of the new believers, but I couldn't shake the picture God had given me of the bungee chord holding us fast. I knew His promise that He would never leave me or forsake me and believed it.

What happened next was nothing short of amazing. Some of our least efficient workers started quitting, and every single person hired in their places happened to be amazing! The quality of our service immediately improved.

And then, the ideas started flowing. Before the time of prayer and thanksgiving, we had three ideas that slightly impacted sales. But, after our prayer, we had about twelve ideas that all had a significant effect, but they required action; on their own, they were nothing. Action required sacrifice. It was hard work to implement the plans we felt God had given us, but worth it.

There was one idea that I knew I just couldn't get behind. It was voiced by a myriad of people who all understood what it takes for restaurants to succeed, my manager being the latest one. "Why don't you just open on Sundays? You know that you're missing out on big sales by staying closed."

My response was always the same. "I can't. I would rather honor God with that day…that sacrifice…than bring in the extra sales."

My manager shook his head. "Maybe God doesn't even care if you do that anymore. You should ask Him again and see if He changes His mind."

I chuckled at that, "If God changed His mind I am sure he would let me know."

At the end of October, our church does what they call a Hoedown, just after the morning services. Basically, the party is meant to be an alternative to Halloween. It is a huge event with hundreds of volunteers and thousands of people coming to join in the fun. These days our kids volunteer there, but back then they were still little enough to get excited about the games and candy.

Kristin and I met some friends of ours in the parking lot after church and organized ourselves a kind of tailgating party for Hoedown. As we were chowing down, I was introduced to a guy who had a restaurant in a neighboring town. When he found out that I also owned restaurants here in Murfreesboro, he started asking questions.

"The thing is," he explained, "We're not doing so well. I could really use some advice."

In the past, I would have been a little judgmental, assuming that his downturn in business had to be his own fault. Now my heart broke for him.

"Do you think you could come see my place? It might give you an idea of where we're going wrong."

"Sure, of course. Happy to," I agreed, all the while thinking, *You don't want my help, buddy. You have no idea how badly my own place is doing.*

As I walked into his restaurant a few days later, I immediately spotted some things that needed fixing. That was a relief. I was worried I would have no suggestions.

"You know," he said toward the end of our visit. "There is one decision I made that really seems to be working out in our favor. We just started opening for breakfast. I was paying staff to be there in the morning to prep anyway, I might as well bring in a few more staff and make some sales."

I had considered opening for breakfast before, but I had never wanted to do it. It seemed like too much of a pain. But this time, it just struck me as a good idea. I too have so many prep workers in the morning, it really wouldn't take much to make the necessary changes.

And I was desperate. What more could we lose? I knew I had to pray about it. I was tired of failing on my own understanding. That night I prayed, looking for clarity at least. I went to sleep, still uncertain if it was a God-given idea or if I was just grasping at straws.

The next morning, I was praying in the shower when a verse came to me, and I started writing it on the foggy glass door. Oddly, I was writing in cursive, and I never did that. The verse began with the word "now." And with just that word, I knew I needed to move on the breakfast idea right away.

I wasn't keen on bringing in a whole bunch of breakfast items. We would create a simple breakfast menu with ingredients we already had plus up to five more items. We'd need jelly for toast, that was a given. But I thought I would just see what we could work with.

I took a tour of our food storage and started to develop a menu. Within an hour I had a breakfast menu that was one of the largest anywhere in Murfreesboro. Dozens of omelets and various styles of eggs benedict, all made from ingredients we already had on hand. I brought the completed menu to management and staff to ask them what they thought. They got excited. This just might work!

Right away, we got on the phone with our distributors so that we could add new items to our order. We printed our breakfast menu, adding our diverse breakfast options. Amongst our current staff, we already had people capable of running with the breakfast service. We only needed to add one server and one host. Breakfast was never going to bring in huge profits, but it would help decrease our costs.

By the time we had everything up and running for breakfasts, it was January—make it or break it time.

We opened with a bang! New customers, who weren't

willing to risk their time or money on a lunch or dinner, were willing to try eating breakfast with us. They liked the breakfasts so much they came back in the evening!

The real proof of success came at the end of February. For the first time, I got a call from accounts payable that we didn't need to hold any checks back that month. We had gotten past the time that the loaned money was designed to get us through. Things were beginning to look up!

I never imagined that God would save us through a mechanism that I said I would never do—breakfast. As I was learning, and I have seen multiple times since then, I should never put God in a box. He will always pull you out as long as you allow Him to work within your life in ways that you cannot imagine. That's what makes Him God and that's what makes me not.

FIFTEEN

Praying in Public

Do you know how good, pure fresh air feels after you have been drowning? Serving breakfast enabled us to keep our heads above water. We were doggy paddling with no land in sight but compared to where we had been three or four months before, we were doing well. I could breathe. Peter D's was now building, instead of continually fixing and repairing.

It was right around this time that I got a phone call from a friend of mine, who had recently been elected Mayor of Murfreesboro. He had run for office at the same time as Peter D's was being built, which is quite a feat as he also happened to be our contractor, and you already know the multitude of issues we ran into with the plans.

"Peter? I have a job for you."

I was listening, curious about what exactly I could do for him. "I was hoping you would agree to come and pray at the mayor's prayer breakfast on the National Day of Prayer."

I'd heard of the prayer breakfast, but I had never attended one before. It had only been a year since I had given my life to the Lord, and unsurprisingly, I had never felt inclined to attend as an unbeliever. Every year Greenhouse Ministries, a group who help the homeless get back on their feet, organized this event. Community members come together, and various speakers pray on a variety of topics modeled after the National Day of Prayer.

"I'd like you to pray for families. It doesn't have to be super long."

"Families?" If anything, I had expected to be asked to pray for business. This threw me for a loop.

"I-I suppose I could. Yes. I'd be happy to."

My heart was hammering, had I really just said yes? I was excited to be asked, but I had rarely prayed out loud, let alone in a room full of people. I would probably stutter and stammer through the whole thing, but something in me compelled me to say yes.

I hung up from the call and immediately felt a sense of panic. Pray for families? Pray what exactly? I opened my laptop and googled, *Prayers for the family*. Surely thousands of other people had prayed for families and lived to post about it. I opened a link—

It read, "Oh, God of love and comfort, in Thy magnificent mercy—"

That sounded nothing like me. I clicked on another site.

"Lord of life, You shape us in your image, and by Your gracious gift the human family is increased—" it began.

Nope, still not what I was looking for. Some of these prayers didn't even make sense to me. I read a few from the National Day of Prayer and other public gatherings, but nothing seemed to fit the situation.

Finally, instead of trying to do it by myself, I decided to go for a walk and pray about it.

"God, You know what I should be praying for. Please help me focus on the right topics. Show me what You would have us pray together at the breakfast."

Apparently, God was just waiting to be asked; as soon as I finished praying, all sorts of issues came to mind that affect families today. I grabbed a pen and started writing. Abuse, pornography, absentee parents, there were even things I had never thought of before; sports, media... In minutes I had a list of almost fifteen different topics.

Looking at my list later, I realized there were a lot of controversial topics, but then shouldn't we be praying for controversial things? Controversies tend to elicit a response because they come with certain moral choices. If anything, they should be the things focused on, especially if they affect our families.

I began to write, my thoughts and prayers flowing out onto the page. I wanted to make sure I organized what I wanted to say so that the attendees could really pray along with me. Once I abandoned the more scripted prayers I had found and sincerely prayed for families and the struggles that come with it, I could start to see how God would lead it. I went for another walk outdoors, praying over the topics I felt God had given me in the same way I had written it down.

As I prayed, one sentence I had written leaped out at me. It definitely needed tweaking. I prayed about it, working and re-working it until I settled on, "Please, do not let the thoughts of man or the idea of political correctness pervert what You set forth for us...."

As it happened, right around this same time the Supreme Court was voting on whether or not to legalize same sex marriage. But to me, the sanctity of marriage went far beyond just this vote. I had recently heard about a woman in Germany who wanted to marry a piece of the Berlin wall. To me, apart from being weird, that was also wrong. Anything that worked against God's original design for marriage was wrong.

At the same time, I didn't want to condemn with words an entire group of people. I didn't want to misspeak and have someone else, unfamiliar with the topic, feel like I was condemning them. I was not. One day, I will face Jesus, and He will sort out my sins, just like everyone else. It is definitely not my place to condemn, but I could ask God to get involved and lead me in the prayer that it would be a true reflection of His desires for the family.

I arrived at the venue a little early. There were easily a hundred and fifty people there. I shot Kristin a text, "I am so scared. I want to sprint out the door."

It may sound like an exaggeration, but it wasn't.

As Kristin was messaging me back, comforting me, a man sat down in the chair beside mine and introduced himself. He was also one of the speakers and was going to talk about health. Unlike myself, he wasn't nervously gripping any sheets of paper.

"Did you have a hard time writing out your prayer?" I asked, assuming he must have it written down somewhere.

He shook his head, "I don't believe in writing out prayers. I pray Spirit-led prayers."

That sounded like a great idea, but it sent me into a whole new flap of nerves. Should I have just winged it? By writing it out, was I doing it all wrong? Does this mean my prayer was not led by the Spirit? I felt it was, but now my inexperience as a Christian was playing with my mind.

I continued to text Kristin, fear at the heart of each message. At one overly dramatic point, I may have even used the word "flee." Each time, Kristin talked me down, comforting me ever while getting the kids ready for school.

The emcee took the podium and introduced the first speaker. There would be several others before it was my turn. My nervousness grew as each, in their turn, spoke and prayed about a variety of topics.

"And now, I'd like to invite Mr. Peter Demos to come and pray for the family."

The emcee had called my name, so I had no choice but to ascend the few stairs to the stage and take my place behind the podium. I assessed the size of the crowd. I usually didn't worry about audience size anymore. Five people or a thousand, it really made no difference. But today it did.

And then, to make it worse, I looked over at a table to my right that had people from my church including my pastor and two associate pastors, all whom I love, and I knew they loved me. And, then they smiled up at me, a very proud smile, but this started freaking me out more.

Oh, my goodness, my pastor is going to judge me on my prayer!

I was thankful I had written it out, after all. If I hadn't, I probably wouldn't have been able to say a thing. I started with an introduction, quoting James McDonald from Harvest Bible Chapel in Chicago, a favorite online pastor of mine, whose program "Walking the Word" has often blessed me.

"Pastor James McDonald said, 'when the devil attacks he's going to attack the church and the family.' I believe he is absolutely right."

I carried on, systematically praying through the topics and the words that God gave me. When I finished, I hurried back to my seat, relieved it was all over and seemed to have gone pretty well.

The man who had sat down with me earlier stood next. I

was curious just what he would cover in his Spirit-led prayer. His microphone wasn't working well for him, but you could pick up some of what he was saying. He started out praying for the health of the nation and all the things that accompany those concerns. I was only halfway listening, to be honest, still trying to calm the adrenaline surge that had hit my body when I took to the stage. But then this man caught me off guard. He started talking about homosexuality and said, quite literally, "Homosexuality is a virus."

It was quite a statement to make in a public forum. I thought some of the topics I had covered were controversial, but this man had just kicked at the proverbial hornet's nest. I was curious about how it would be received.

"Peter? I just wanted to say thank you for your prayer earlier."

A young man in a dark suit walked alongside me after the breakfast.

"I can't tell you how much it meant to me, but God knows."

As people started to leave, others from the audience came with similar comments. I have to admit, it felt pretty good. I congratulated myself on nailing it. My pastor later told me that it was a prayer that would convict pastors! I was so proud of myself.

I wanted to rush home and tell my wife how it all went, but I had an urgent meeting right away with my dad and sister about family business matters so debriefing with Kristin would have to wait.

Instead, I called her, "Honey, I nailed it!"

"That's great! Well done. I am happy for you. Will you be home soon then?"

"Yes, but if you need to get ahold of me, you'll have to call the office. I'm gonna turn off my cell for the meeting."

By the time I got home to Kristin that evening, the adrenaline from the morning had worn off, and I really just wanted to talk over what my family and I had discussed in our business meeting. It was the most current news, and the meeting had the most potential conflict that day. We sat on the porch together and happily chatted over all that was said and done.

We were just heading back inside when I realized my phone was still off. When I turned it back on, it started to vibrate, and several message alerts buzzed in quick succession. I opened the newest message from Greenhouse Ministries director, Cliff Sharp. It said, "I'm sorry this is happening to you."

Sorry what was happening to me?

I scrolled up to the original message. It included a picture of me. A bad one. I didn't have time to read what it said when my phone started to vibrate once more. Texts, emails, messages, they all started pouring in.

"Oh, my goodness, have you seen this..." was the usual tag line, many including links to the article by a local news journal.

It was the same article Cliff had sent me, with the horrible picture of me at the top. I was in the middle of saying something, but the side profile shot made me look like I was screaming at someone. The headline read, "Gay Marriage a Hot Topic at Mayor's Prayer Breakfast."

The report incorrectly quoted me throughout the article. But most shockingly, the words spoken by the man who followed me, "Homosexuality is a virus," although not attributed to me, was referenced in such a way that combined with my picture, it made it look like at first glance that my entire prayer was me screaming at people wanting to kill every homosexual in the land.

The reporter, who I had previously considered a close acquaintance, never talked to me once before running the article. He never requested a copy of the prayer I had written out from anyone. It was a surprise attack. I was caught completely off-guard, and making matters worse, the article was far from accurate. It stung. He and I had talked many times over the previous year. He had even come to my defense over a zoning problem Peter D's had with the city.

The fear of having to close the restaurant was still niggling at me in the background. We had just about overcome our biggest obstacles and criticisms but in one day—BAM! All our arduous work was obliterated.

I skimmed through this libelous material and felt helpless against it. In the old days, I would have had lawyers and a PR team on it before ten minutes was up. But this time I really felt I had to trust God to fight for me instead. I started texting every believer I knew around the world, asking for prayer. God would fight for me, I need only be still (Exodus 14:14).

The one thing I learned from everything that had happened with Peter D's so far is that God would not let me hit the rocks below. He held me secure. Sure, I was worried about what might happen to Peter D's and Demos', several other businesses had closed across the nation over the topic of gay marriage, but I knew that God was in control and I could trust Him.

Then came the big attacks, and they were vicious! All over the internet, netizens began to tear us to shreds. Articles, reviews, and comments were all aimed at taking down the "hateful Peter Demos."

Some of our close non-Christian friends did all they could to distance themselves from it, even as loads of Christians, people that I barely knew, came to our defense.

Next came the BOYCOTT DEMOS' and PETER D's Facebook page. It was started by a guy in Memphis, four hours away, who not only quoted an already libelous article full of untruths, but he got the quotes wrong! That didn't matter to his followers. The page started racking up likes.

Employees threatened to walk out, some wore rainbow ties as a protest; I didn't even realize they were doing this until I complimented someone on their colorful tie (I have always been a fan of colorful ties). Some of our gay employees stopped me to ask me about it, "I know this isn't you...but I just need to be sure. I'm losing friends for defending you."

I was grateful my employees wanted to confirm and set the record straight instead of jumping on the bandwagon with everyone else. But I felt terrible that they were suffering on my behalf.

People that accused me of being hateful were threatening to kill me, and several people tweeted out our home address. When that happened, my thoughts went immediately to Kristin and our two young children who like to play outside in the yard.

This was becoming a safety concern. "I think we need to put out the truth at least," Kristin said one day as we were talking about it. "I'm going to message the Boycott Demos' Facebook page and give them a copy of your speech."

She not only gave them a written copy of the speech, she also gave them a link to the audio when the newspaper released it to the general populace, assuming that it should clean things up. Instead, they did their best to twist and manipulate those words into an attack. I shouldn't have been surprised. In fact, I wasn't surprised at all.

Kristin and I prayed continuously, asking God to protect us, our children, and our business. We talked to our children about how to deal with these types of attacks, teaching them how to deflect anyone who said anything by telling them they need to talk straight to us. At least this could be a teachable moment.

One night, as we were praying as a family, our daughter, Karys, prayed, asking God to forgive all those who were persecuting us. My heart swelled. Then our son, Jamey, prayed that God would bless those who were persecuting us.

I had never been so proud of my kids. That should have been my prayer all along, but it hadn't been. I had just been praying for this whole nightmare to stop.

The next day, Kristin called the newspaper to set up a meeting. When we arrived, the editor and some guy that looked very much like a lawyer were there waiting. Their body language shouted that they were ready for a fight. We sat down across from them, and Kristin began by sharing the inaccuracies in the article.

I tried to stay above the fray, but my carnal nature caused me to make a couple of sarcastic digs, "Do you realize," I chimed in, "That there was a quote in the article, that ended with the words 'Peter suggested'? I'm just curious…how you can suggest a quote. It seems to me a quote is something directly stated, not implied."

That felt good. I had another…

"I'm surprised that with the bad grammar, an editor

looked at the article and did not catch it or consult a Harbrace textbook."

Okay, maybe not my most stellar of moments, but staying quiet in a fight is hard!

We went on tell them all about the problems that arose as a result of the misinformation they'd published, and the potential fall out from closing.

"Do you understand what would happen if you close us down?" Kristin asked. "All the employees that will be out of a job...all the charities that won't be helped? There are some very real consequences here."

At this point in the conversation, the editor started to look sad, and she refused to look at us for long periods of time. The lawyer man, on the other hand, didn't seem to care a lick. His face remained very stoic. Finally, he asked the question that had been bothering him, "I don't understand, what do you want?"

It was apparent that he was still waiting for a fight to start. I smiled. He had failed to realize, we weren't here to pick a fight.

"I guess I want to thank you," I said.

That totally confused the two of them.

"Look, I want to tell you about something that happened with my kids recently."

That got them to look me in the eyes. In fact, it got them staring, obviously curious about what I was getting at.

"We were praying together as a family, and my son and daughter prayed something that blew me away. My daughter asked God to forgive the people that were hurting us, and my son asked God to bless them. I couldn't have taught them that lesson if this hadn't happened. We now understand why God used the Chaldeans in Habakkuk, and we just really want to thank you."

I didn't think they would get the Habakkuk reference, but maybe they would look it up. To our surprise, tears sprang up in the editor's eyes, and the lawyer man gaped at us in disbelief. Kristin and I shook their hands and left the tiny newsroom that used to be home to a much larger publication. We had done what we had to do. Everything else was in God's hands.

The most incredible thing happened after that meeting. Everything just stopped as if a switch was flipped! By going to the newspaper and saying we weren't going to fight and by saying thank you for the lesson learned, it was like the weight lifted. The Facebook page never got another follower. The online comments ceased; there were no more nasty tweets, no more hateful messages.

Our business didn't die off; it continued to move forward slowly. In fact, we never suffered any real consequence apart from the stress of the incident itself.

For a couple of years, we didn't advertise with the newspaper that had run that original article, but today, God has helped us to forgive enough to go back.

On occasion, someone will ask about it, but for the most part, things just worked out. It proved to me again that God will not forsake us, and He doesn't leave us where we were. Sometimes God does not get rid of a problem entirely; but at the very least, He allows a moment of relief right when we need it.

It's amazing, watching what happens when I speak out for Christ today. I know that at any time we could be cast back into the fray. We may again face dramatic persecution for our beliefs. But I have noticed that when anything negative threatens, God gives me moments of rest. He lays a table before me in the presence of my enemies (Psalm 23). He offers rest even at the mouth of a lion (Daniel 6:22).

Sixteen

Winning

Do you like being afraid? The amount of money Hollywood invests in horror movies suggests that many people do. But not me. I hate it. I've had too many years living as a slave to fear. When God became Lord of my life and dealt with those fears, it was a part of my rebirth. I loved living in the freedom and power that comes when God's Holy Spirit lives in you. But when everything started going wrong, and it seemed like the whole world (or at least the entire population of Tennessee) was against my family and me, I was back in that battle.

After everything that had happened as a result of my prayer at the mayor's prayer breakfast, it was tempting to keep my beliefs a little more in the background than I had been. I allowed fear of persecution to paralyze me for a time.

I believe that fear is born out of a lack of trust. I had to ask myself, "Do I trust God's promise to protect me? Do I trust the Word of God when He says that He has given me the resources freely and asks me to give as freely as I received?"

How many times in the Bible does God call us to be courageous? I've done a quick, not exhaustive, count, and it adds up to more than one hundred times!

From what I can see, courage is not the absence of fear. There are many stories of brave soldiers who despite fear, acted courageously and earned themselves medals of honor.

We tend to assume that if we are following after God, He will simply pick us up and move us out of whatever scary situation we are facing. But the truth is, journeying with Him up to the mountain top often starts in the valley. As David explained from one such valley experience, "You prepare a table before me in the presence of my enemies...my cup overflows." It takes a lot of courage to sit down and eat rather than stand up and fight when enemies are closing in.

Kristin and I had learned a lot about trusting God to fight for us in these last few years. Even today, as I write this, we are in a time when we have to trust God to work on our behalf.

We discovered a few months back that one of our general managers had been stealing from us, and we had to let them go. Another long term manager walked out in the middle of a shift, informing us he would be opening his own catering and BBQ place. The sting of that betrayal was aggravated by the fact that this was a man we had walked with through many personal battles within his family.

Around that same time, we had a company offer to take over the building for Peter D's and lease it from us. The deal made perfect sense financially, but Kristin and I felt a bit like we were taking our only son to the top of Mount Moriah to make a sacrifice to God.

It hasn't been easy to let go of control and allow God to lead us. Sometimes, as we've walked through a valley, it was hard to imagine that sitting just above, hidden by the clouds, are the mountain tops. We remind ourselves, they are not so far out of reach if we focus on following the Shepherd instead of focusing on, and being paralyzed by dark shadows.

Running a Christ-centered business doesn't make you immune from making mistakes or from the mistakes of others. It takes strength and courage to rest in Him. It is easier to let fear paralyze you; outwardly this may look similar to waiting, but there is no rest in fear. There is no "waiting on God."

Although it has been a hard week, my wife and I can see that God is fighting for us and that helps relax and rest. We don't know what we will do as far as Peter D's is concerned, but we do know we cannot thwart God's plan, but we can look forward to our future, knowing that as we trust in God, He will guide us.

Second Timothy 1:7 tells us that "For God has not given us a spirit of fear, but of power and of love and of a sound mind."

When I look at actual failures in my life, they all stem from my attempts to protect and preserve, rather than trust and take risks. It is only after God strips everything away and we are left only with Him that we discover He is more than enough. Jesus only is all we need.

Some may look at my life and ask, "Who are you to talk about fear and failure? When have you ever failed? Sure, things went wrong for a little while but look at how it all turned around. You've got a house and a car. You've got the perfect nuclear family. You have your own business. When did you ever really fail?"

And fair enough, from outward appearances it may look like that. But as I grow in my relationship with Christ, I learn more and more that He sees success and failure very differently than the way the world looks at it.

Success is generally defined by how much money you

have, how much stuff you own, how many fans you have accumulated, or how much power you yield. But this success is always temporary.

No matter how successful you are in this world, you will eventually die. King Solomon, arguably the wisest and richest man that ever lived wrote this: "I have seen all the works that are done under the sun; and indeed, all is vanity and grasping for the wind" (Eccl. 1:14). This man, who had it all, knew how unsatisfying wealth, power, and an endless supply of concubines really was.

Successful comedic actor Jim Carrey famously said, "I think everybody should get rich and famous and do everything they ever dreamed of, so they can see that it's not the answer." In another interview, he's quoted as saying, "Everything you gain in life will rot and fall apart, and all that will be left of you is what was in your heart."

He was arguably at the top of his game when he chose to walk away and live a quieter life, focusing instead on charitable work. From what I can tell, he still hasn't found Jesus, but he seems to be searching in the right direction.

So how does God define success? What is the purpose He has for us? What does He ask us to do? Is He asking us to live a life of poverty and prudence? Maybe some individuals are called to this, but there are some whom God has called to live out their faith in affluence.

I played a lot of sports in my childhood. In certain sports, I stunk. I just couldn't get the hang of it. I looked like a newborn foal trying to find its legs. In others, I did reasonably well, some might even say I had a talent for them. However, even during my best years, and at the height of my skill during my best game, it was clear that I had no chance of becoming successful at a professional or even a collegiate level.

What you learn in sports, is that success can be measured on a multitude of levels. Each has its own scoring and rules. What might bring you success in one sport would be ruinous in another. You would never play golf the way you do basketball. If you had the same score in golf as you did in basketball, you would be failing miserably.

The success of a sports team is usually determined by their scores and their win/loss record. But in some cases, it can even be defined by one game. It has often been joked about that Auburn could lose every other football game of the season, but if they beat Alabama, it would be considered a successful season by the fans.

In other words, success is defined differently based on who creates the game, who defines the rules, and who is cheering you on. It is achieved by accomplishing the purpose of what you are meant to do.

Does God ask us to convert everyone who crosses our paths in a day? Am I more successful than you if I lead ten people to the Lord in a day, and you convert one in a decade? Are you more of a success if you memorize the whole of the New Testament while I struggle with just learning Psalm 23? Of course not!

Shortly after I was saved, I had an opportunity to tell my story to a large number of people. Because the majority of these people were Christians, or at least curious and wanting to understand how Jesus changed my life, I received a tremendous amount of encouragement. That reassurance felt pretty good. It gave me a lot of courage to keep going and keep being really open about my new-found faith.

It was a little while later when I received an online complaint from a MTSU professor about Peter D's, telling me that he would never eat with us because we were too open about our faith. Now, this was not the first letter I had received like this, and it was far from the last, but as had become my habit, I offered to meet and discuss this with him, fully expecting that he would reject me as all the others had.

Imagine my surprise when he wrote back to say that we should meet at a local coffee house for our discussion. A conversation like this could go a couple of ways. It could be that he agreed to meet so that he could tear a strip off me in person. But it could also be, I surmised, that God was doing something in his heart, and this was just an opportunity to lead him to faith. This filled me with nervous excitement. Would he be aggressive as he implied in his online post, or would he be respectful? Not that it mattered either way, I knew that God sent me to talk to him and so I would go.

I showed up early, ordered myself a coffee, and waited. He showed up a few minutes later, no pitchfork-wielding mobs followed him in, so I figured I was safe.

Once we were both comfortably sipping our coffees, I proceeded to share my story with him. And let me tell you, I was on fire. I don't think I have ever recounted my story so clearly or with as much animation and enthusiasm as I did in conversation with this man. I was thrilled, knowing that God was using me to tell a non-believer, who was openly hostile to Christians, all about who He is and how He transforms lives.

When I finished my story, I looked at the man with wide-eyed expectancy. He tilted his head a little, meeting my gaze. "Your story did not move me at all."

That heart-wrenching sentence was delivered with zero

emotion. There was no hint of a smile, but nor was there any animosity. There was just...nothing. No reaction.

Sometimes naiveté can be a great protector of your emotions. Instead of being offended, I went into my old college debate mode. "Can I ask you your objections to Christianity? Is there something in your past that makes you feel this way?"

I mean, if he was not emotionally moved, then maybe he could be convinced logically.

In the course of our discussion, it came up that he was Jewish and had been offended by Christians in the past. I always hate to hear that. I told him about my love for Israel and tried to express my understanding of the history of the Christian persecution of Jews.

But he didn't seem interested in that and quickly switched topics, explaining that he was actually a humanist. He started quoting old school philosophers and seemed genuinely surprised that I had read several of them. It was clear he intended to intimidate me.

Despite that, our discussion was very cordial, and it seemed to me that we were developing a friendship. I was wrong. When I tried to email and follow up on our coffee talk, he responded with a brief, "Good fences make great neighbors."

I replied, with a word of caution, "Whatever fence you build to protect you from the outside, also will fence in. Be careful what stays inside the fence."

As much as the professor's words might have offended me in the past, they had the opposite effect now. My heart was for this man. I desperately wanted him to be my brother in Christ, which is why one of his later statements cut deep.

He said, "All you care about is converting others so that you can have another notch on your belt."

At the time, this was not my intent. I really was just excited about the opportunity to share my story and my faith, but his statement haunted me for years. I felt like I failed God. It wasn't that I was looking for a conversion, but I had hoped to soften him somewhat. He seemed to have left just as lost as when he came. So, was this a failure?

In this world, if my business doesn't make sales, it would be considered a failure, but how does God see this? If success is defined as an accomplishing your intended purpose, then it begs the question— what am I meant to do?

Jesus tells us that we are to be His witnesses when the Holy Spirit comes down on us. So one thing to be counted as a success in God's kingdom is when we bear witness to His life at work in us.

When the disciples asked Jesus, Who will be greatest in your kingdom? Jesus called over a child, pointed to them and said, Whoever humbles themselves like this little child will be the greatest.

And later, when the mother of two of His disciples came to ask Him to let her sons sit on his right and left when He came into His kingdom (positions that would denote success), He told her that whoever wants to be great in God's kingdom needs to be a servant of all. Whoever wants to be first, must become a slave.

He didn't say, Whoever has the most knowledge of scripture. He mentioned nothing of converts, nor did he mention finance. The thing needing to be great to be a "success" in God's kingdom is almost the polar opposite of what the world counts as great.

It wasn't my job to make a convert of the professor. If I made him a convert, I would have failed my mission. My purpose and my responsibility was to share the Gospel. It is only God who can change a heart. Once the Gospel is shared, the onus is on the listener to respond. It is their free choice to say yes or no to Jesus.

So…success is sharing. Not converting. Every chance I can, I try to share the Gospel. I do not want to thump people over the head with it, but I do want to present opportunities for people to know who Jesus is so that they might find salvation. If I am blessed to witness that moment take place, awesome!

But with the majority of the people I witness to, I see little response. As far as I am aware, there have been ten people who have accepted Christ into their hearts at our restaurants. I know there is likely more out there but whether I find out about them or not is of lesser importance. What really matters is that we take every opportunity to share the hope that we have in Christ.

Is that the only way to be successful in God's kingdom? Not at all! Not only are we all called to be witnesses for Christ, God has also given every person specific gifts and talents. It is our job to be intentional in using these abilities. Not only do we fail if we don't use them, we actually deserved to be punished.

I believe that our restaurants really belong to God, and in order to serve and glorify Him through them, we need to make it an avenue for spreading the Gospel, not that we want to hit people over the head with it. We don't have a rubber stamp in the back to tally up the converts. Like it says in 1 Peter, we want to take every opportunity to give an answer for the hope that we have…with gentleness and respect. To do this, we implemented changes, some of which were very obvious, and some that were a little more subtle, allowing us to share if people asked.

If you walk into one of our restaurants today, you will find a little table in our lobby with small Gideon New Testaments for people to grab, free of charge. We don't say much about it. The books are just there, and people can take one or not. Since we started putting them there, we have had thousands taken, and we pray that they will be read.

Walking into Peter D's, you would notice a wall of fancy looking clocks, each set to different times. They weren't put there to tell you the time of cities around the world. They don't even have batteries in them. If you flip each clock over, you will see that there is a book of the Bible written on the back. The clock set to 3:16 has John written on the back of it. Each clock is set to our favorite Bible verses.

Originally, this was something that we had done just for me, a fun little secret. But we had so many people ask what it means, we began to see the opportunity it created to share God's Word. Now we have a little diagram of the clocks, with the corresponding Bible verses for each printed on a piece of card paper to hand to anyone who asks about them. We've had the opportunity to pray for many staff and customers because one of those verses was exactly what they needed at the time.

Prayer matters, y'all. I know that when I choose to try and fix problems myself, success is not guaranteed. But if I pray, trusting God's leading, we always end up right where He wants us to be.

This is why we pray out loud before our meetings, we

host volunteer prayer meetings, we take prayer requests from staff in both our evaluations as well as with a sheet hanging on the wall. We encourage people to pray for healing and comfort.

Recently, we asked our customers and employees to participate in a prayer to offset the hatred that was coming to one of our cities through a racist march and protest. We knew that prayer matters, and that God could shut down these hateful actions. He tells us not to be overcome by evil but to overcome evil with good. So, we handed out cards to every one of our customers encouraging them to pray. On the scheduled day of the protests, they canceled the event because they were confused. God answered!

When possible, we try to use these types of life lessons and lessons from the Bible to help coach and encourage our staff in their personal and professional lives. Once I started reading the Bible every day for myself, I was shocked at the number of answers I found to everyday problems. I try to pass this on as well.

I mentioned before that our general manager meetings open with prayer, positive focus, and a devotion; and we host a weekly Bible study that all employees are welcome to attend.

We've hosted or sponsored all sorts of Christian events and encourage all employees to come to them by paying for their tickets, and on some occasions, help cover their shifts if we can. We've been blessed to have great speakers come to our community: Lee Strobel talking about the movie *Case for Christ;* radio host and prolific author Eric Metaxas; Angus Buchan and Allen Jackson, who were instrumental in my coming to Christ. And so many more.

The chaplains we hired from Corporate Chaplains of America to serve our staff and their families are on call 24 hours a day, seven days a week. They stop by one to two times a week to visit with employees, but the amount of calls they receive is incredible.

In less than three years, they have made six jail visits, eleven funerals and weddings, sixty hospital visits, more than six thousand one-on-one Care sessions, and have made contact with our employees 62,176 times!

And we have our Ambassador, who daily shares his story of salvation and restoration, counseling others while he works alongside them, training and prepping them for work in the company.

When I look at it, I suppose there is a similarity between business success and God's success. Regardless of talents and gifting, no business, no athlete, no one has ever succeeded if they were afraid to take a risk. Risk doesn't guarantee success, but it provides an opportunity for it.

Earlier I mentioned that there were some sports I tried that just were beyond me. Soccer was one of those. When I started playing soccer, I was terrible. I seemed to have no co-ordination in my feet. In the 14 years I played, I scored only one goal the day I had my shoes on the wrong feet. In all likelihood the ball had probably bounced in an unexpected way, landing it in the net.

There was one game we played when our starting goalie was sick, and the backup goalie got hurt. The coach looked at me and the other kid sitting on the sidelines playing with grass, and realizing that the other kid was worse than me, decided to put me in. It felt like a risk. I had never played in goal before.

I suppose the greater risk in this situation belonged to the coach, but fortunately, it paid off for both of us. I was fearless in the net. I enjoyed getting banged around to protect my goal. I was so successful, I took over the starting job for that season and never played in the field again.

My lack of fear kept my team from losing many times. I got kicked, headbutted, and ran into the post from time to time, but it didn't stop me. This was my thing. This was where I excelled until one game changed all of that.

The opposing team kicked the ball over my defenders and outran them to get to the ball, making it a head to head matchup. I decided to stay back on the line, instead of charging the ball. It was the wrong choice. I couldn't keep up with them all, and they scored on me very easily. I was fuming. How could I have made a mistake like that?

A minute later, I had the same opportunity. The ball was kicked in the same position over the same defenders, and the same forward was chasing the ball. I was determined that they were not going to score again! This time I charged ahead.

As I ran, I could see that my opposition was slightly faster than I anticipated. I dove for the ball and knocked it out of the way at the same time he pulled his leg back to kick. Instead of connecting with the ball, his foot landed on another round object—my head. He knocked one of my teeth directly behind another.

I came to, moments later, to see paramedics running across the field to help me. When I recovered and could play again, things were different. I was afraid of getting kicked in the head, and rightly so. But because of that fear, I became a horrible goalie. I never played again.

This same type of fear happens to us as Christians when we have a terrible experience while sharing our faith. Many of us couch our fear by hiding behind this quote, famously attributed to St. Francis of Assisi, "Share the Gospel at all times, and when necessary, use words."

Imagine four men each doing the same good deeds, and each one for different reasons. One of those men is being led by Christ to act, but how does anyone know this unless he uses words? How is he "preaching the Gospel" by keeping his motivation to himself? He cannot!

The Bible is pretty clear about this.

How then shall they call on Him in whom they have not believed? And how shall they believe in Him of whom they have not heard? And how shall they hear without a preacher? And how shall they preach unless they are sent? (Romans 10:14-16).

Now then, we are ambassadors for Christ, as though God were pleading through us: we implore you on Christ's behalf, be reconciled to God (2 Corinthians 5:20).)

It can feel a little scary at first. I used to be one of those people that made it hard for Christians to share their faith, I know! But I am so grateful to the ones who tried and through both speech and action, repeatedly pointed me to Christ.

Have I've been rejected when I shared? Yes! You read my earlier story.

Have I been laughed at? Yes!

Have I seen people get to know Christ? Yes!

And I believe in each of those situations I met with equal success because ultimately my purpose was being met. God was being honored and testified about.

When I was receiving the hate mail from people after the

mayor's prayer breakfast, I found another email in my inbox from the MTSU professor, and my heart nearly stopped. He decided to pry up a corner of that fence he had erected and emailed me.

I couldn't even open his email when I first saw it, expecting it to tell me that, my "hate" was what keeps him from being a Christian. It took me a full twenty-four hours to work up the courage to click on the tab. And then several more seconds to comprehend what he was saying.

It wasn't an angry email at all. In fact, it was very encouraging. He told me how unhappy he was with the article, and although it was clear he was not a Christian, he stood up for me. Out of all of the support I received, this was the most heartening of them all.

The impact we have on people lasts beyond what we can see. I hope I can encourage you to act boldly. It is my prayer that as we continue to share the Gospel, we have the privilege of seeing a revival in our world.

Trust in God. He will not let you down.

EPILOGUE

And we know that all things work together for good to those who love God, to those who are the called according to His purpose (Romans 8:28).

Peter D's has closed its doors. We had limped along, hoping things would get better, literally pouring our blood, sweat, and tears into the place. There were many successes, like the addition of breakfast, among other things, that brought us hope and helped us to carry on as we learned the lessons God wanted us to learn. In the end, it seems that journey of faith has been more important than the actual on-going success of the business.

As I mentioned before, Peter D's had been limping along when we received a call from a restaurant company asking if we would be interested in leasing our building. My first instinct was to respond with a solid no. We had worked so hard, and things were slowly starting to look up. But never in all my years in the restaurant business had anyone called with a request like this. It was so out of the blue, I knew it was important we talk to God about it and see if this offer was part of His plan.

When I talked first to Kristin about it, she cried at the thought of closing up shop on Peter D's after so much time and effort to keep it open. I then took the proposal to my executive team, to hear their thoughts.

"It does bring in more income with a fraction of the effort. You at least need to give it your full consideration" was the unanimous consensus.

It was such a big decision I still felt the need for more confirmation. I called up Pastor Allen and asked his opinion. He also agreed it was good deal, but what clinched it was when I met with Trent, my C12 chair. The C12 is a group of Christian business owners in the area that meet once a month to discuss our businesses and ministries.

Trent, in a matter-of-fact sort of way, reminded me, "You can't thwart God's plans. If He wants it to happen, it's going to happen one way or another. If He doesn't want this deal to go through, He will stop it."

"Okay..." I reluctantly agreed, "I guess we'll wait on God and see what He does with this."

And that is exactly what we did. We waited. And waited. The company made several visits to the building, often with only a few minutes notice. I would give them a tour and answer their countless questions. They would promise to get back to me, and I would wait some more.

It can be very frustrating to wait on God's timing, and this was no different. The old Peter would have called them to push things through, but I knew that ultimately, I wanted to know God's will and that meant letting Him work and not interfering in the process.

It got to a point where I was under pressure to make some time sensitive decisions. We had a contract renewal coming up on billboard advertising, and we needed to hire a new manager if we were going to stay open.

I was at a soccer game with my son when the stress of waiting got to be too much for me. I had a responsibility to keep things running smoothly if we didn't end up leasing out the building. I climbed to the top of the stands to make my call. It was a very cold Spring day, the wind was strong, and it was hard to hear, but I did catch these words clearly: "We actually have another building in Murfreesboro that we're interested in. That's what has been holding us up. Can you give us to the last week in March to let you know one way or the other?"

It wasn't the definitive answer I was hoping to hear. I thought of all the ways I could convince them to choose our building instead of the other, a surprising reaction considering how upsetting the idea had been to me in the beginning. I was actually kind of disappointed.

"You can't thwart God's plans." Pastor Trent's words came back to me.

So, unlike me, I did precisely what I needed to do. I waited. Time passed, the deadline passed, and I realized that the deal was not going to happen.

My brain was working out all sorts of plans to make Peter D's better. I had to do my best to fix our problems. I needed to make a plan. I went into work to have a good look. I knew that we had to be fanatical about everything from the back of the kitchen to make it better in the front.

We'd start in the prep rooms, that would help us fix problems we had slowing us down in the kitchen. And there are less moving parts in the back; a recipe doesn't change if you follow it correctly.

So, I walked in and started by looking at every prep item. Even if it looked good and tasted good, if it was not perfect or made with our exact procedure, I would scratch it off. By the end of the day, I had removed eighteen items from the menu while the employees scrambled to remake them the right way and get them back on it.

I pulled out of Peter D's onto Medical Center Parkway, a

major road that runs through Murfreesboro, heading for the office.

Like King David in many of his Psalms, I felt helplessness and hope battle in my heart. I wasn't even sure how to pray about it anymore. With all the lessons I have learned, I knew in my mind that God had this. He was going to turn Peter D's around, or the deal would have gone through. My heart felt heavy at my inability to see His answer, but I knew it was there.

I arrived at the office a few minutes later to God's surprising answer.

"Peter!" my controller greeted me. "We had a call from David at McAllister's Deli, while you were out. He was asking to lease the building!"

"McAllister's?" I was flabbergasted.

In fact, I burst out laughing. Never, in all my years in the restaurant business, had I received a request to lease a building, and now we had received a second request in only three months?

"Yes, David at McAllister's. He asked if you could call him back," she confirmed.

When I called David back, it became clear that God was continuing to lead us in this direction.

"I don't know why," he explained, "but I just felt I needed to call and ask if there was at least a possibility."

"I'm not going to say no, but isn't our building a little too big for your needs?" Our restaurant was about twice the size of McAllister's current place.

"Oh, I can go big. I'm not worried about that; and the truth is, every time I drive by your building, I just get the feeling that I need to ask."

Within one week, we worked out the initial terms, quickly signed a lease agreement, and by the end of the month, Peter D's would close. We had to get all our food, equipment, décor, and everything else out of there so that McAllister's could take over the space.

I've noticed, that as God continues to ask me to put things into His hands, I start out with faith and confidence that He will work things out for the best. But it never seems to happen quickly enough for me. Inevitably, I grow impatient and disappointment creeps in, and it is only then that God shows up and does what He was going to do.

The extra months lost during the negotiations with the first company gave us time to develop PDK Southern Kitchen and Pantry—a fresh idea, taking many items from our menu developed for Peter D's and recreating them for a fast, takeaway style restaurant.

Our Reuben sandwich, chicken tenders, and in-house ranch dressing could all be brought over. We had time to develop several other items to suit PDK's Fast Casual concept: shrimp and grits, freshly caught salmon, fried chicken, and more. We could take equipment from Peter D's and put it into PDK, making sure it fit this time and reducing the start-up costs.

All the battles and frustrations we'd experienced with Peter D's, we could role play and fix at PDK.

With the opening of PDK, we decided on a specific prayer strategy, based on a Bible Study we'd been working through, by the Kendrick Brothers, *A Battle Plan for Prayer*. The question posed in the book was if God said He would answer yes to every prayer you prayed for a week, would you pray generally or specifically? You would be specific, wouldn't you? We started to get specific, and as we did, we found that God did answer yes to 95% of those prayers. His answers were clear and precise, just as we had been.

There were problems with Peter D's I just couldn't fix, and I can praise God for that. During a recent conversation with our pastor, he asked me what I learned through this experience, and my answer is quite simple. Through the journey with Peter D's, God freed from my pride.

In the four years it was open, if it had become a raving success, I would have taken credit. I would have been proud that I had struggled through and made it better than anyone had predicted. If it failed in six months, I would not have learned to lean on Him with endurance. God's taking that pride away has helped me see that I can't thwart His plans. The things that God wants to accomplish in my life, He will accomplish.

It reminds me of the story of Esther, when Mordecai tells the new queen, if it isn't you, it will be someone else. But what will happen to you if you don't follow the will of God?

I risk missing out on so much blessing if I fail to follow God's leading.

I had an opportunity to hear Lance Lambert, an international Bible teacher, speak about living in Jerusalem before he passed away. His talk focused on the prophecies in Ezekiel. He said, "I'm not worried about living in Jerusalem, because I know from God's Word what will happen to it. God's hand of protection is on that city."

And that is how it should be for our lives too. As children of the living God, we can live in the freedom of knowing God's protection is on us. Even if our physical bodies fail, we have an assurance of eternal life.

It's amazing to look back at prophecies about historic places like Babylon. They wrote things in faith that must have seemed absurd. It would be like someone in the 1600s writing that the newly minted United States of America would become a major global superpower. But for us, having the opportunity to look back into history, we can see God's hand at work, and it is awesome. We can see how things lined up perfectly and how God used people and situations that seemed irredeemable to teach and bless us, leading us deeper into a relationship with Him.

Kristin was very emotional when we first spoke about closing Peter D's. Our last day open, she cried a lot. It was really hard for her. It was hard for both of us. Driving by the empty building with the Peter D's sign no longer there was a little heartbreaking. But now, not many months later, she would tell you quite honestly that she doesn't really miss it anymore. She doesn't even really think about it.

She hadn't realized at the time what a burden it was. Now that the weight of it is lifted, she can move forward with joy. She has a tremendously healthy attitude towards life in general.

I feel the same. It has been some hard lessons, but I wouldn't trade this time of learning and growth.

As I write, PDK is in its second day of training. We open in less than two weeks. We just did a test run and were able to get all the food out in six minutes. Fresh and fast—such a difference from our Peter D's trials four years ago.

We are moving into a new chapter with the freedom of knowing that PDK Southern Kitchen and Pantry is 100% God's. He can close it if He wants to. But if He keeps it open, I will run it faithfully as His steward.

About the Author

President and CEO of Demos' brands, and D's Seas, Peter Demos has food service coursing through his veins, having grown up in his parents' restaurants. After becoming a lawyer, he turned back to his heart's calling, the hospitality industry.

Today Peter is a successful restaurateur with four Demos' Restaurant locations, two PDK Southern Kitchen and Pantry restaurants, and Peter D's catering, offering a lineup of authentic dishes the family spent many years developing. His restaurants operate with a mission-oriented approach that is radically different in the fast-paced food industry.

Peter believes that risk and faith open doors to success, and he shares the challenges he encountered while navigating failures and overcoming fears as a business owner. He believes values come first, creating unique training techniques and positions supporting values as a business priority. These management decisions may oppose traditional business methods but have proven to make a difference in the lives of his employees and create a healthy working environment that makes for better service overall.

Peter is a speaker who inspires business owners and people of all walks of life to lead others with courage and purpose. He currently resides in Murfreesboro, Tennessee, with his wife and two children.

To obtain more information about Peter Demos,
or to request him to speak to your group,
please visit the website www.afraidtotrust.com.

To purchase some of the products
that Peter Demos uses in his restaurants,
please visit: www.demosfamilykitchen.com